Nicl

Get going with Kindle Fire

covers the standard LCD and HD models

In easy steps is an imprint of In Easy Steps Limited
4 Chapel Court · 42 Holly Walk · Leamington Spa
Warwickshire · United Kingdom · CV32 4YS
www.ineasysteps.com

In Easy Steps Limited supports The Forest Stewardship Council (FSC), the leading international forest certification organization. All our titles that are printed on Greenpeace approved FSC certified paper carry the FSC logo.

MIX
Paper from responsible sources
FSC® C020837

Printed and bound in the United Kingdom

ISBN 978-1-84078-587-6

Contents

1 Kindling your imagination. 5
About the Kindle Fire 6
Kindle Fire specifications 7
Buttons and ports 8
Setting up your Kindle Fire 9
Battery and charging 10
Changing the Kindle's name 11
Shopping on the Kindle 12
Using the Amazon Cloud 13
Amazon Prime 14

2 In your Kindle element 15
The Carousel 16
Navigation Bar 18
Home button 20
Back button 21
Status Bar 22
Quick Settings 23
Kindle Fire Settings 24
Screen rotation 26
Searching your Kindle Fire 27
Adding Favorites 28

3 Starting up the Cloud Drive 29
Accessing the Cloud Drive 30
Adding content to the Cloud Drive 31
Using the Cloud Drive App 32
Cloud Drive photos 35
Cloud Drive documents 37
About Cloud and Device 40

4 Inspiring with apps 41
About Kindle Fire apps 42
Finding apps 44
Downloading apps 46
Deleting apps 47
Apps Settings 48
Must-have apps 50

5 Lighting up entertainment 51
Launching the Cloud Player 52
Uploading music 53
Transferring music 55
Managing your music 56
Creating a playlist 57
Playing music 58
Viewing your own videos 60
Viewing movies and more 62
Issues with video 63
Sharing photos 64

6 Igniting a passion for reading 65
Obtaining books 66
Book Settings 68
Reading aloud 69
Thumbing through books 70
Adding Notes and Bookmarks 72
Sharing your thoughts 74
Finding Definitions 75
Turning on the X-Ray 76

7 **Bringing the Web to life...77**

Browsing on the Kindle Fire.......78
Getting Silky..............................79
Opening pages...........................80
Finding your way around...........81
Bookmarking pages 82
Links and images 83
Adding tabs 84
History and Reader.....................85
Silk Settings 86

8 **Keep the flame burning... 87**

Adding email accounts 88
Working with email 90
Adding contacts.........................92
Using calendars..........................94
Contacting with Skype...............96
Linking to social networks 98

9 **Don't get burnt................ 99**

Parental Controls......................100
Locking your Kindle Fire...........102
Location-based Services 103
Privacy issues............................104

1 Kindling your imagination

The tablet computer market is becoming increasingly competitive and the Kindle Fire is fast establishing itself as a significant player in this arena. This chapter introduces the Kindle Fire, shows how to set it up and details what it can do. It also covers the role of Amazon, which is integral to the Kindle Fire, as most of the content comes from Amazon and the online cloud service, Amazon Cloud Drive.

About the Kindle Fire

Mobility is now a key word in the world of computing, and tablet computers are beginning to play a significant role in how we all communicate and access information. The Kindle Fire is a fully-fledged tablet that has evolved out of the Kindle eReader that was originally designed for reading books, newspapers and magazines. The Kindle Fire takes this several steps further, with functionality to:

- Surf the Web and access your favorite social networking sites
- Use email
- Listen to music
- Download apps
- Play games
- Watch movies
- Read all of your favorite books

One of the first things to say about the Kindle Fire is that it is an Amazon product and most things on it are linked to Amazon in one way or another. To use the Kindle Fire you need to have an Amazon Account with a username and password. If you do not already have one this will be set up if you buy your Kindle Fire from the Amazon website or, if you buy it from another retailer, you can create an Amazon Account during the setup process. Most of the content in terms of books, movies, music and apps comes from Amazon, although there are some items that you can also upload to your Kindle Fire.

The Kindle Fire has a standard model and an HD model: both have a 7 inch screen (in the US there is also an 8.9 inch HD version) and a minimum of 8 GB of storage so it is powerful enough to be able to store the content you need, whether at home or on the move.

Kindle Fire specifications

The specifications for the Kindle Fire HD and standard Kindle Fire are:

- 7 inch (diagonally) 1280 x 800 pixel HD display (1024 x 600 pixels on the Kindle Fire) with polarizing filter and anti-glare technology. There is also a border around the viewing area
- Dolby audio and dual-driver stereo speakers (Kindle Fire HD) or standard stereo speakers (Kindle Fire)
- Dual antenna, dual-band Wi-Fi for fast downloads and HD streaming (Kindle Fire HD), single band Wi-Fi (Kindle Fire)
- 1.2 Ghz dual-core processor with Imagination PowerVR 3D graphics core for fast and fluid performance (Kindle Fire HD), or standard 1.2 Ghz processor (Kindle Fire)
- 8 GB storage (Kindle Fire) or 16 GB or 32 GB (Kindle Fire HD), plus free unlimited cloud storage for all of your Amazon content (see Chapter Three for details)
- Front facing HD camera for free Skype-to-Skype calls (Kindle Fire HD only). To use this to take photos you need the HD Camera app
- An HDMI port for viewing your content on your TV or other devices (Kindle Fire HD only)
- Up to 11 hours battery life (Kindle Fire HD, 9 hours for the Kindle Fire) for mixed use including reading and surfing the Web

Don't forget

In the US there is also an 8.9 inch version of the Kindle Fire HD available. This has a 1920 x 1200 HD display, a 1.5 GHz processor and the top of the line version has 4G Wi-Fi connectivity.

Buttons and ports

The buttons and ports on the Kindle Fire are located along the edges of the device and consist of:

- On/Off button. Press this once to turn on the Kindle Fire or put it into sleep mode. Press and hold to turn it off
- Volume buttons
- Stereo jack, for use with headphones or to connect to a stereo system
- Micro-B Connector for charging the Kindle Fire. This connects with a USB port on a computer or the Kindle Powerfast Charger (sold separately from the Kindle Fire)
- Micro-HDMI Connector for connecting the Kindle Fire to a high definition TV (Kindle Fire HD only)

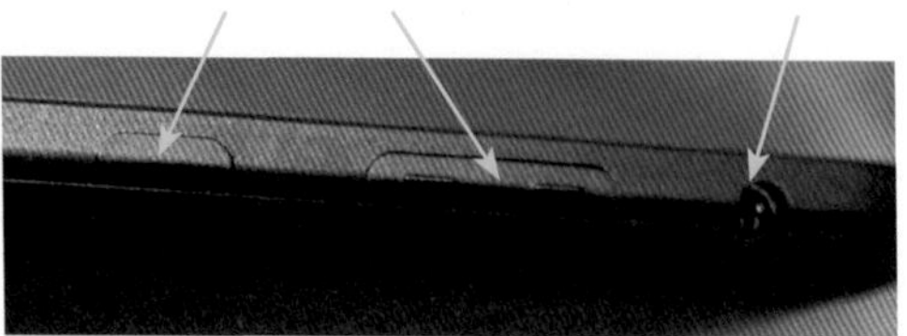

Setting up your Kindle Fire

When you first turn on your Kindle Fire you will be taken through the setup process. This only takes a few minutes and once it has been completed you will be ready to use your Kindle Fire and all of the related Amazon services. The elements of the setup process are:

- Select a language (tap on the Continue button after each step)
- Select your Wi-Fi connection (this can also be done at a later time). Your home Wi-Fi should show up for selection at this point
- Register your Kindle Fire with your Amazon Account, or create a new Amazon Account
- Select your time zone
- Link to your Facebook and Twitter accounts (this is optional)

Once you have completed the setup, your Kindle Fire will be ready for use; there are no other system requirements. The first thing you will see is the Kindle Fire Home screen which is in the form of the Carousel. See Chapter Two for more information about using this. There is also a Lock Screen that is activated when the Kindle Fire is put to sleep. This contains promotions from Amazon and can be turned off for a fee of US $15 (UK £10) *(correct at the time of printing)*. Drag the padlock to the left to access the Carousel from the Lock Screen.

Battery and charging

Battery life is important for any tablet device and the Kindle Fire can be used for up to nine hours from a single charge (11 hours for the Kindle Fire HD) for general use such as surfing the Web, reading, listening to music and viewing videos. It comes with a Micro-B Connector that can be used to charge the Kindle Fire. There are two options for this:

- **Charging with a separate AC Adapter.** This comes in the form of the Kindle Powerfast adapter, which has to be bought separately from the Kindle Fire. The Micro-B Connector attaches to the adapter with a USB connector and the adapter can then be plugged into the mains power
- **Charging with a computer.** The Kindle Fire can also be charged by connecting the USB end of the Micro-B Connector to a Windows or Mac computer. However, this takes longer to charge than the Powerfast adapter

The Kindle Fire HD charges in approximately four hours using the Powerfast adapter, but up to 13.5 hours if it is connected to a computer via a USB port. The Kindle Fire charges in approximately three hours with the Powerfast adapter and 11.5 hours if it is connected to a computer.

The Kindle Fire charges more quickly if it is in sleep mode and even more quickly if it is turned off. However, it can still be used as normal while it is being charged, if required.

Hot tip

One useful app that can be downloaded from the Amazon Appstore is the Battery HD app. This displays a selection of information such as how long you can use the Kindle Fire for different functions and how long until charging is completed.

Changing the Kindle's name

When you initially set up your Kindle Fire it will be given a default name based on your own Amazon Account name, e.g. Nick's Kindle Fire. This is displayed in the top left-hand corner on the Status Bar at the top of the screen. However this can be changed to anything of your own choosing. To do this:

1. Log in to your online Amazon Account

2. Under the **Your Account** heading, click on the **Manage Your Kindle** link from the available options

3. In the **Your Kindle Account** section click on the **Manage Your Devices** link

Your Kindle Account

Manage Your Devices

4. Click on the **Edit** button next to the required device

5. Enter a new name and click on the **Update** button. The new name will now appear on the Status Bar on your device

Shopping on the Kindle

The Kindle Fire is an Amazon product and it is unashamedly linked to a wide range of content from the Amazon website. This include books, games, apps and music. This can all be accessed from the Shop button on the top Navigation Bar. To do this:

1. Tap on the **Shop** button at the top of the Kindle Fire window. (This can also be accessed using the Store button from individual sections)

2. The main Shop window contains a rotating range of promotional items. Tap on the buttons at the bottom of the window to view specific categories

3. Content can be downloaded for specific categories such as Apps, Books and Games

4. Enter a keyword in the Search box to find items across all of the Stores

Using the Amazon Cloud

Another integral part of the Kindle Fire is the Amazon Cloud. This is available on the Amazon website once you have bought a Kindle Fire and consists of:

- **The Cloud** for storing content that has been purchased from Amazon. This includes items such as ebooks and music that have been bought from Amazon. Once this is done, the content is not only available on your Kindle Fire, it is also stored, free of charge, in the Amazon Cloud. All of your compatible purchased content is stored in this way and it can then be downloaded to other Kindles, or by the Kindle app on other tablets and smartphones
- **The Amazon Cloud Drive.** This can be used to upload your own content, including photos, music and documents, which will then be available on your Kindle Fire. You get 5 GB of free storage in the Amazon Cloud Drive but you can buy additional space if required
- **The Cloud Drive Desktop App.** This is an app that can be downloaded to make it easier to add content to your Cloud Drive. You do not have to use it, as you can upload content directly to the Cloud Drive, but it makes the process easier and can be used on Windows and Mac computers. You will be prompted to download the Desktop App when you start to upload content through the Cloud Drive
- **The Cloud Player.** This can be used to upload your own music, which will then be available on the Kindle Fire. It can be downloaded from the Cloud Drive and then the Amazon Music Importer can be used to scan your computer for music to upload

For more information about using the Amazon Cloud see Chapter Three.

Amazon Prime

When you buy a Kindle Fire you are entitled to a free month's trial of the Amazon Prime service. This consists of a virtual lending library where you can borrow one book a month, free of charge and with no due dates. You also get unlimited free two-day delivery (US, one-day in the UK) on Amazon items. To use Amazon Prime for borrowing books:

1. Tap on the **Books** link on the main Navigation Bar on the Home screen

   Books

2. Tap on the **Store** button

   Store >

3. Tap on the **Kindle Owners' Lending Library** link under the **Categories** heading

4. Tap on a title to view details about it

5. Tap on the **Borrow for Free** button to download the title to your Kindle Fire

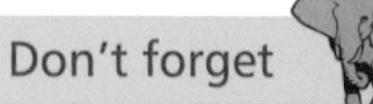

Don't forget

The Amazon Prime service in the US also includes the streaming of movies and TV shows. The cost for Amazon Prime is US $79 (UK £49) per year *(correct at the time of printing)*.

2 In your Kindle element

The Kindle Fire is, literally, a very hands-on experience. This chapter shows how to quickly get to grips with the interface and controls of your Kindle Fire so that you can begin accessing, downloading and using the wide range of available content. It also details how you can search over your Kindle Fire and save your most commonly-used items as favorites.

The Carousel

After the Kindle Fire has been turned on, and the Lock Screen opened, the first thing you will see is the Home screen. This is in the format of a Carousel with a line of icons for accessing various apps and libraries:

1. Swipe left and right to move between items on the Carousel

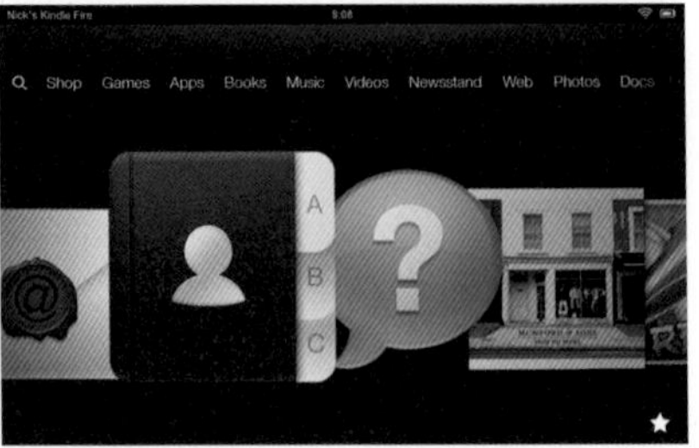

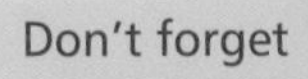

The Carousel displays the most recently-accessed items, so its appearance will change on a regular basis.

2 Change the orientation of the Kindle to view Quick Links buttons at the bottom of the screen. This can also include recommendations from Amazon (this feature can be turned off in **Settings > Applications > Amazon Home Recommendations** and tap on the **Hide** button)

3 The most recently-opened item is displayed at the left-hand side of the Carousel

4 Tap and hold an icon on the Carousel to access its menu. This can be used to add it to your Favorites list, remove it from the Carousel, or, if applicable, remove it from the Kindle Fire completely

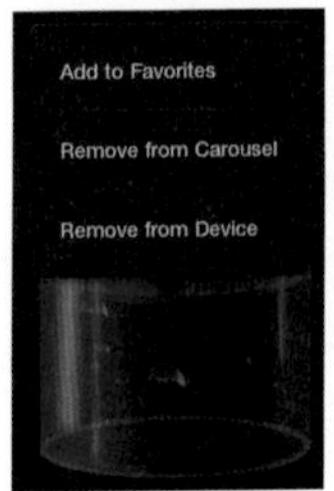

Navigation Bar

The Navigation Bar at the top of the Home screen contains links to all of the main content libraries on the Kindle Fire. To use this:

1. Swipe left and right to view all of the library headings

2. Tap on a link to go to that library

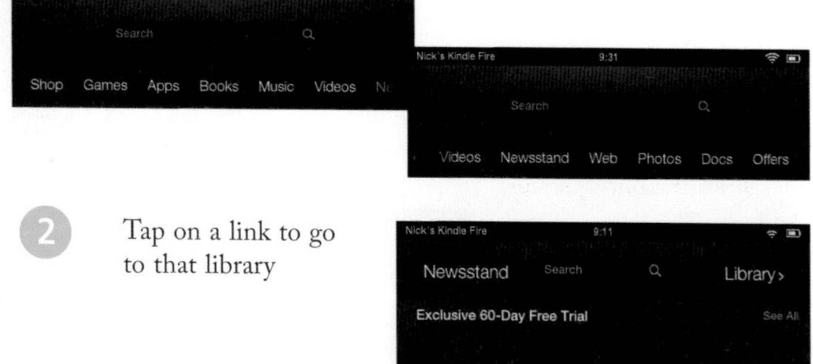

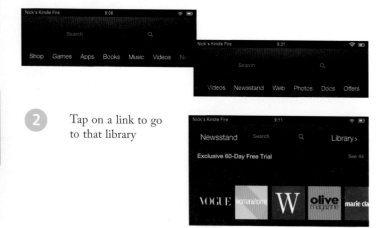

The content libraries on the Navigation Bar are:

- **Shop.** This takes you to the Amazon website where you can buy and download content for your Kindle Fire
- **Games.** This section contains the games that are stored on your Kindle Fire. If more games are downloaded they will be located here
- **Apps.** This is where your Kindle Fire apps are located and where new apps can be downloaded to

- **Books.** This section stores the Kindle books which you have downloaded. You can also view books that are not on your Kindle yet, but stored in the Amazon Cloud. When you access them in the Cloud they are automatically downloaded onto your Kindle Fire
- **Audiobooks.** In the US, this option is available for audiobooks from Audible.com
- **Music.** This section contains the music that you have bought from Amazon, or downloaded from your own computer
- **Videos.** This is where you can access, download and view videos from an online provider
- **Newsstand.** This is where you can download newspapers and magazines and take out subscriptions for the latest editions
- **Web.** This accesses the Web, using the Kindle Fire's own web browser, Silk
- **Photos.** This is where you can view photos that have been uploaded to the Amazon Cloud Drive, or copied to your Kindle Fire
- **Docs.** This is where you can use documents that have been uploaded to the Amazon Cloud Drive, or copied to your Kindle Fire
- **Offers.** This is where you can view offers from Amazon. These are the items that also appear on the Lock Screen

Hot tip

Use the Personal Videos app in the Apps library to view your own videos. Connect your Kindle Fire to the computer and copy the videos into the **Movies** directory within the file structure.

Home button

When you are navigating around the Kindle Fire, it is important to be able to get back to the Home screen as quickly as possible. This is done by tapping on the Home button, which appears on the **Options Bar**, which is on every screen apart from the Home screen. The Home button takes you directly back to the Carousel.

1. In landscape mode the Home button is located at the bottom of the Options Bar

2. In portrait mode the Home button is located at the left-hand side of the Options Bar

3. Tap on the **Home** button to go back to the Home screen (Carousel) at any point

Don't forget

When you are surfing the Web on the Kindle Fire, the Home button takes you back to the Carousel, not a web home page.

Back button

In addition to the Home button, another important element in navigating around the Kindle Fire is the Back button. This is also located on the **Options Bar**. It is used to go back to the most recently-visited page in whichever library, or app, that you are currently using. To use the Back button:

1. Open an app or go to one of the main libraries on the Kindle Fire. The Back button is located in the middle of the Options Bar in both landscape and portrait mode

2. Tap on the **Back** button to go back up to the next level. If you are at the start screen of an app or a library this will take you back to the Home screen

3. Tap on an item within a category

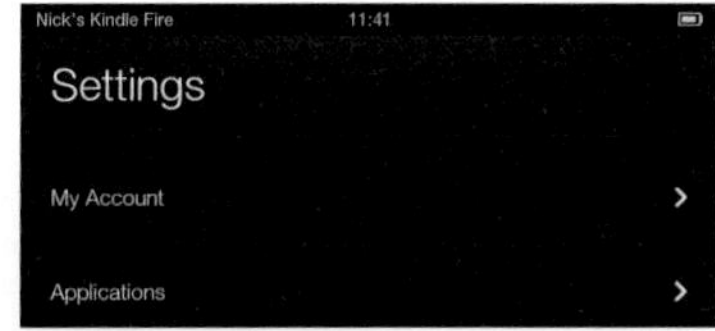

4. Tap on the **Back** button to go back to the previous level in the selected category

Status Bar

The Status Bar is displayed along the top of the Kindle Fire's screen and is visible all of the time.

The Status Bar contains various items, including:

- Your Kindle Fire's friendly name
- The current time
- The status of your Wi-Fi connection (and Bluetooth if used)
- The charge status of the battery

Additional settings can also be accessed from the Status Bar, by swiping downwards from any point on it. This displays the Quick Settings (see page 23), Notifications and an option for accessing additional Kindle Fire Settings (see pages 24–25).

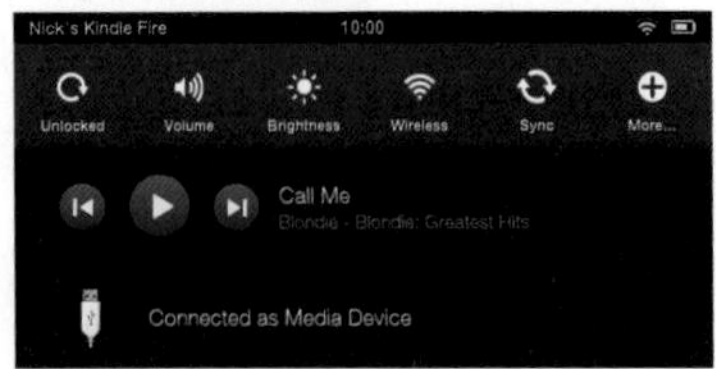

Don't forget

The expanded Status Bar also shows details of any running apps and if the Kindle is connected for charging.

Quick Settings

When the Status Bar is expanded, by swiping down on it, the Quick Settings are available below the items on the previous page. These are:

- **Lock/Unlock screen rotation** (see page 26)
- **Volume.** Use this to change the system volume (this can also be done with the volume buttons on the body of the Kindle Fire)
- **Brightness.** This changes the screen brightness. (The lower the screen brightness, the less battery power will be used)
- **Wireless.** Use this to access settings for connecting to and managing Wi-Fi and Bluetooth connections
- **Sync.** Use this to synchronize your Amazon Cloud content with your Kindle Fire
- **More.** Use this to access the full range of Kindle Fire Settings

Tap on one of the Quick Settings to access options for editing them.

The volume buttons on the body of the Kindle Fire can be a bit fiddly, so it can be easier to use the Quick Settings volume option instead.

Kindle Fire Settings

The More button on the Quick Settings Bar provides access to the full range of Kindle Fire Settings. Tap once on the **More** button to access them:

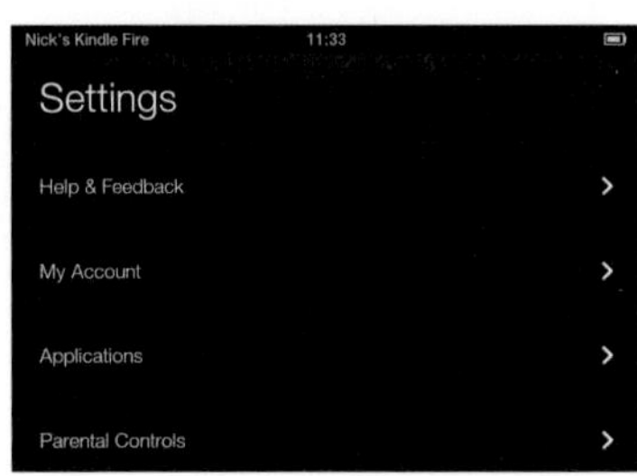

The Kindle Fire Settings are:

- **Help & Feedback.** This offers some information about using your Kindle Fire and also access to the Kindle Support Pages
- **My Account.** This displays information about the registered user including their name and the Kindle email address that would have been created when the Kindle Fire was registered during setup. It also has options for managing your social networking accounts, such as Facebook and Twitter, and also email accounts and contacts
- **Applications.** This contains a range of functions for managing the applications on your Kindle Fire (see Chapter Four for more information about this)
- **Parental Controls.** This can be used to restrict access to certain apps or types of content on the Kindle Fire (see Chapter Nine for more information about this)

- **Sounds & Displays.** This can be used to set the volume on your Kindle Fire, specify sounds for notifications, set the screen brightness and the screen timeout, i.e. how long before the screen goes to sleep if the Kindle Fire is inactive
- **Wireless.** This contains options for managing your Bluetooth and Wi-Fi connections and also for adding new wireless networks
- **Device.** This displays information about your Kindle Fire, including the amount of storage that specific items are taking up, the amount of battery power left, a Date & Time option where you can edit your time zone, disable the installation of apps from unknown sources and resetting your Kindle to its factory settings (if you do this you will lose all of your personal data from your Kindle Fire)
- **Location-Based Services.** This can be used to enable, or disable, apps to use your location as part of their functionality. This is done via Wi-Fi and it can be useful for items such as map apps
- **Language & Keyboard.** This contains options for changing the language used on the Kindle Fire and the format for the keyboard
- **Security.** This includes some advanced security settings and also an option for adding a password to the Lock Screen
- **Legal & Compliance.** This contains details of legal, safety and privacy information

Beware

If you reset your Kindle Fire to its factory settings in the Device section you will lose all of your personal data that has been stored on your Kindle Fire.

Screen rotation

The Kindle Fire screen can be rotated between portrait and landscape and it offers a slightly different screen view for each mode.

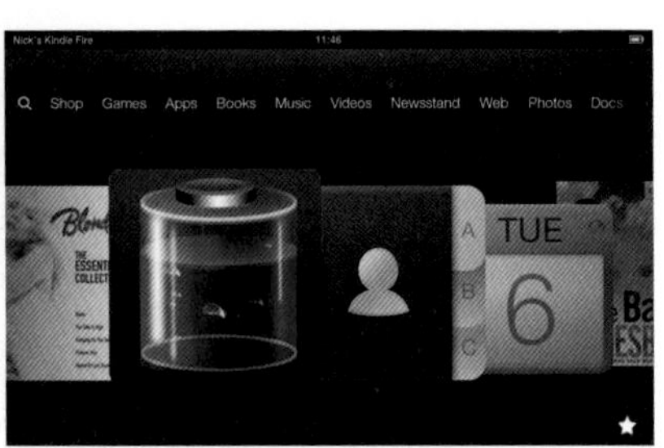

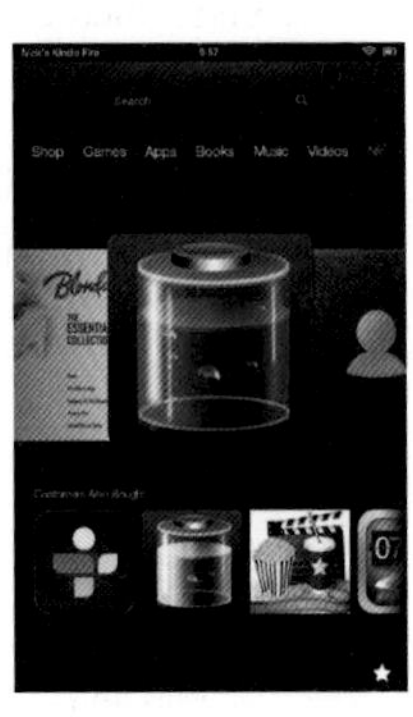

By default, this happen automatically whenever you rotate the screen in your hands. However, there may be times when you want to disable this feature so that the screen in locked in either portrait or landscape mode. To do this:

1. Access the Status Bar. By default this button will display **Unlocked**

2. Tap on the button so that is displays **Locked**. Repeat the process to unlock screen rotation

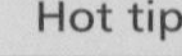

Hot tip

Locking the screen is a good idea if you are reading, so you do not get disturbed by accidentally rotating the screen.

Searching your Kindle Fire

As you acquire more and more content it is important to be able to search over your Kindle Fire to find what you are looking for. Searches can be performed over the Kindle Fire's libraries, the Amazon Store or the web. To do this:

1. On the Home screen, in landscape mode, tap on this button (this is also available from the same Options Bar as the Home button and the Back button)

2. On the Home screen, in portrait mode, the Search box appears above the Navigation Bar

3. Tap in the **Search** box and select whether you want to search over **Libraries**, **Stores** or **Web**

4. Enter a search keyword. Matches will be displayed below the Search box. There will also be options to view Amazon Store and web suggestions

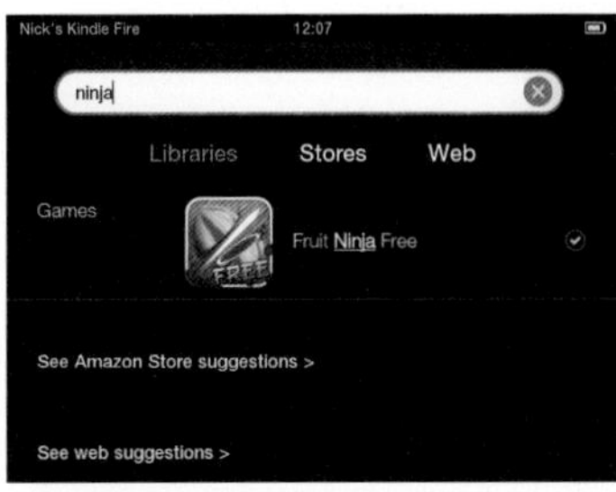

Adding Favorites

We all have our favorite books, music and apps that we go back to time and again. In order to make it quicker to access them, there is a facility on the Kindle Fire to add items to a Favorites panel. They can then be accessed from here with one tap. To do this:

1. Tap and hold on an item on the Carousel and tap on the **Add to Favorites** link

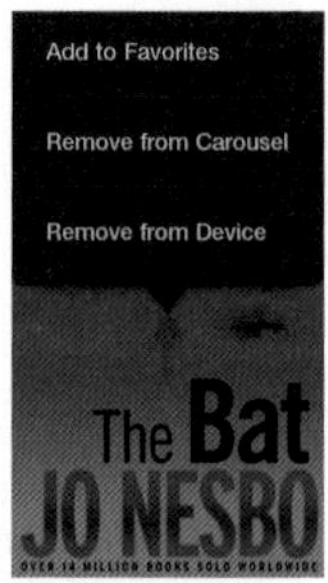

2. Tap on this button to access the Favorites panel (this is available on the same Options Bar as the Home and the Back buttons)

3. Links to all of your Favorites are available in the Favorites panel. Tap on an item to access it

4. To remove an item from the Favorites panel, tap and hold on it and tap on the **Remove From Favorites** link

3 Starting up the Cloud Drive

Cloud computing is becoming an integral part of the digital world and the Kindle Fire embraces this through its close connection with the Amazon Cloud and Cloud Drive. This enables content from the Amazon website to be used on the Kindle Fire, while it is still saved in the Amazon Cloud. This chapter shows how to use the Cloud and also the Cloud Drive to upload your own photos, music and documents and then access them on your Kindle Fire.

Accessing the Cloud Drive

As mentioned in Chapter One, the Amazon Cloud Drive can be used to upload content from your computer. Once this has been done, compatible content will be available on your Kindle Fire.

When you buy a Kindle Fire you will be allocated an Amazon Cloud Drive automatically, with 5 GB of free storage space. This can then be accessed from your Amazon Account. To do this:

1. Access the Amazon website and click on the **Sign in** link to access your Amazon Account with your username and password

2. Under the **Your Account** heading, click on the **Your Cloud Drive** link

3. The Cloud Drive interface is where you can start uploading content from your own computer (see page 31)

Adding content to the Cloud Drive

The default folders in the Cloud Drive are for Photos, Documents and Videos. However, these can be deleted or moved and new folders can also be added, using the **New Folder** button. Content can be uploaded to the Cloud Drive Home page or any of the folders. To do this:

1. Click on one of the folders to access it

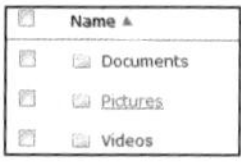

2. Click on the **Upload Files** button

3. You will be prompted to download the Cloud Drive App (see page 32). Click on the **Not at the moment button** to continue without it

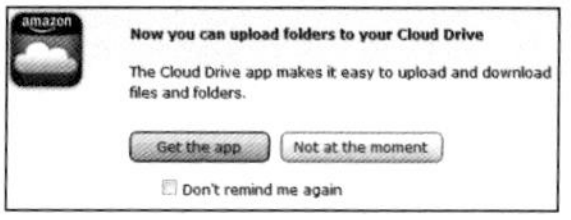

4. Click on the **Select files to upload** button

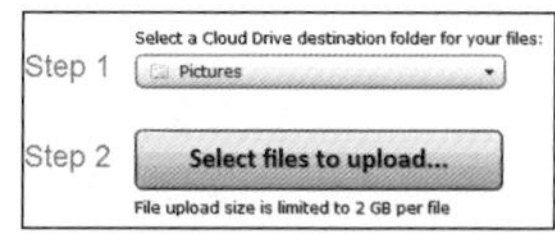

5. Select the files you want to upload

6. Click on the **Open** button. The files will be uploaded to the selected folder in your Cloud Drive

Using the Cloud Drive App

If you want to have a bit more flexibility for uploading files to your Cloud Drive, you can use the Cloud Drive App. This has to be downloaded to your computer and then you can use it to upload your content to the Cloud Drive. To do this:

1. When adding content to your Cloud Drive, click on the **Get the app** button when prompted to download the Cloud Drive App as in Step 3 on page 31

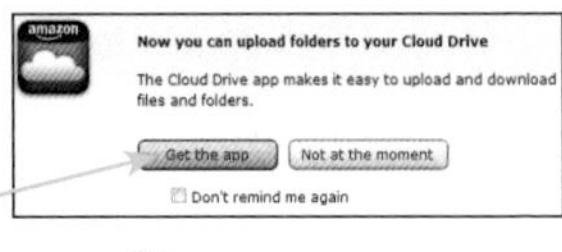

2. Click on the **Save File** button to save the installation file for the Cloud Drive App

3. Double-click on the installation file to launch the Setup Wizard

4. Click on the **Install** button to install the Cloud Drive App

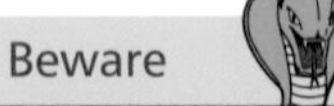

When you install the Cloud Drive App you may be asked for authorization to perform the installation. Click **Yes** at this point.

Uploading with the Cloud Drive App

To upload content with the Cloud Drive App:

1. Click on the **Amazon Cloud Drive** button on your computer

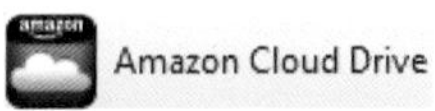

2. The Cloud Drive App has an area where you can drag and drop the files and folders that you want to add to the Cloud Drive

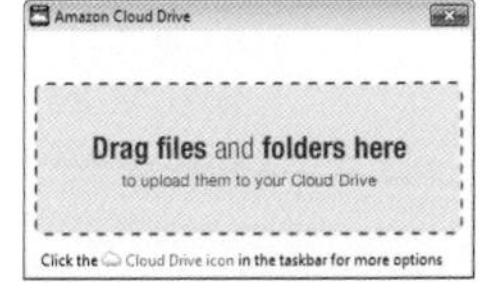

3. When you first drag and drop files and folders into the Cloud Drive App you will need to sign in with your Amazon Account username (email) and password. Click on the **Sign in** button

4. The App indicates that the files are being uploaded

Uploading your files...

5. The files are placed in the **Uploads** folder within the Cloud Drive

...cont'd

6 Click on an item in a Cloud Drive folder to view it

7 Photos are displayed in the Cloud Drive Photo Viewer

8 Check on this box next to a file to perform editing tasks on it

9 Use these buttons to download an item, delete it, move it, copy it, or rename it

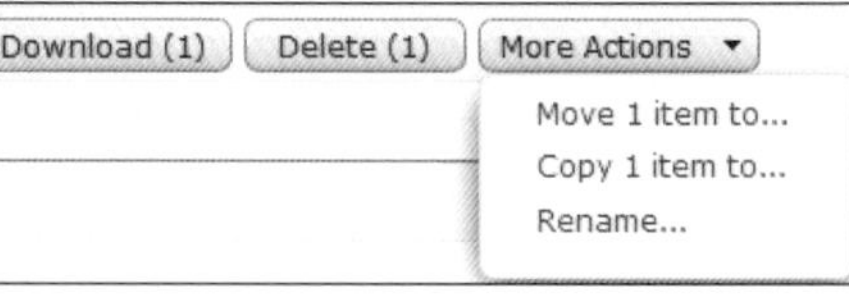

Content can also be uploaded to the Cloud Drive from a removable drive, such as a pen drive.

Cloud Drive photos

Any files can be added to the Cloud Drive, but photos and documents can also be viewed on, and downloaded to, your Kindle Fire.

Although there is a Pictures folder and a Documents folder in the Cloud Drive, photos and documents can be stored anywhere in the Cloud Drive and they will still be available on your Kindle Fire. To access photos from the Cloud Drive, on your Kindle Fire:

1. Tap on the **Photos** button on the main Navigation Bar

   Photos

2. In the Photos app, tap on the **Cloud** button

3. The photos in the Cloud Drive are displayed and this replicates the folders in which they are stored

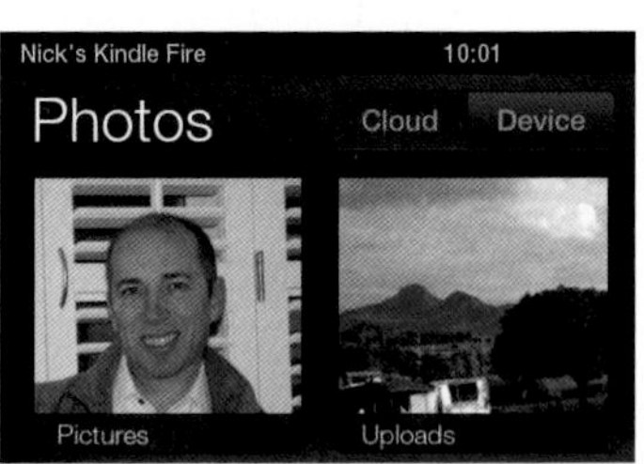

4. Tap on one of the folders to view the photos within it

...cont'd

5 Tap on one of the photos to view it at full size

6 Tap on the **Menu** button on the Options Bar (this is where the Home button and the Back button are also located)

7 Tap on the **Download** button to download the photo onto your Kindle Fire (this has to be done with an active Wi-Fi connection to the Internet)

8 Tap on the **Back** button to go back to the Photos app Home page (you may have to tap on the Back button twice)

9 Tap on the **Device** button

10 The downloaded photo is displayed in the Photos library, within the same folder as in the Cloud Drive. Tap on the folder to view the photos within it

Cloud Drive documents

Certain types of documents can be shared between the Cloud Drive and your Kindle Fire. These include Word, Excel and Powerpoint files and also PDF files. They can be uploaded in a number of ways, including through the Cloud Drive, and then viewed on your Kindle Fire. To do this via Cloud Drive:

1. Upload the files to the Cloud Drive in the same way as for uploading photos. On your Kindle Fire, tap on the **Docs** button on the main Navigation Bar

   Docs

2. Tap on the **Cloud** button to view compatible documents in the Cloud Drive. (If documents are not compatible they will not show up under the Cloud section even if they are in the Cloud Drive)

3. Tap on an item to open it (this will also automatically download it to your Kindle Fire)

4. The document will be opened by an appropriate app on your Kindle Fire (the default pre-installed app is OfficeSuite)

   OfficeSuite

Nick's Kindle Fire 12:31

About Kindle Fire.d... FIND WORD COUNT

About the Kindle Fire

Mobility is now a key word in the world of computing and tablet computers are beginning to play a significant role in how we all communicate and access information. The Kindle Fire is a fully-fledged tablet that has evolved out of the Kindle eReader that was originally designed for reading books, newspapers and magazines. The Kindle Fire takes this several steps further, with functionality to:

...cont'd

More options for adding documents

Two other methods for adding documents to your Kindle Fire are:

- Emailing them to your Amazon email address (this is generated when you first create your Amazon Account and is displayed at the top of the **Docs** library on your Kindle Fire)
- Connect your Kindle Fire to your computer using the Micro-B/ USB Connector and copy documents into the **Documents** folder. To do this:

1. Connect your Kindle Fire to your computer as described above. Locate your Kindle Fire in File Manager (Windows) or Finder (Mac) and click on the **Internal storage** link

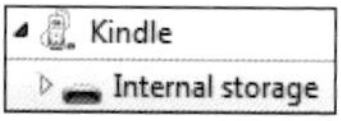

2. Double-click on the **Documents** folder and copy documents here, either by dragging and dropping them from another location or by copying and pasting them. (Other types of content, such as photos, music and videos can also be copied to your Kindle Fire in this way)

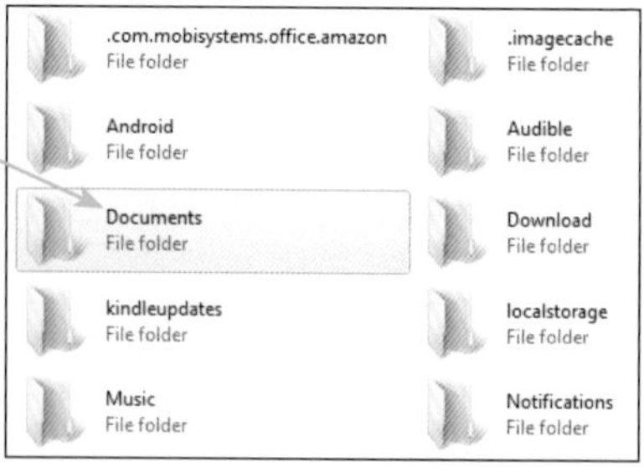

3 Before the file is copied there will be a warning window saying that the file may not be compatible. This appears for all file types, whether they are compatible with the Kindle Fire or not. Click on the **Yes** button

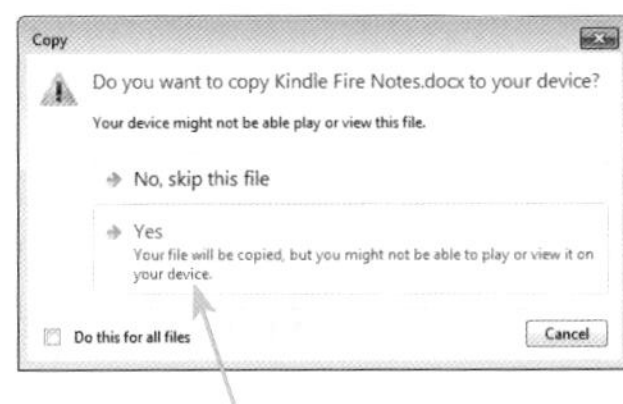

4 The file is copied into the **Documents** folder on your Kindle Fire

5 Tap on the **Docs** button on the main Navigation Bar

6 Tap on the **Device** button to view the item that has been copied in Step 2. This is not available under the **Cloud** button as it is not in the Cloud Drive

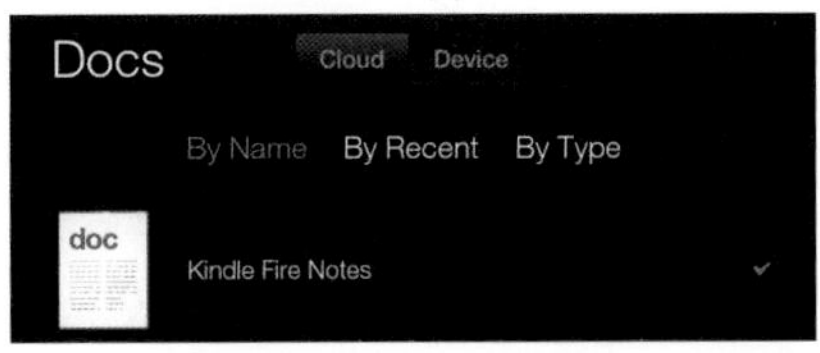

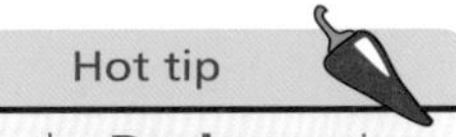

To delete a document, tap and hold on it in the **Device** section and tap on the **Remove from device** button.

About Cloud and Device

The Amazon Cloud plays an important role in the functionality of the Kindle Fire and this is a summary of how the two interact:

- The Cloud is used to store as much content that you have bought from Amazon for your Kindle Fire, e.g. ebooks, music or apps
- The Cloud Drive can be used to upload your own content to be stored here. You get 5 GB of free storage. Photos and documents can then be downloaded to your Kindle Fire from the Cloud Drive

Certain libraries have options for viewing content in the Cloud or on the Device, i.e. your Kindle Fire. The ones with this functionality are:

- Apps
- Books
- Docs
- Games
- Music
- Photos

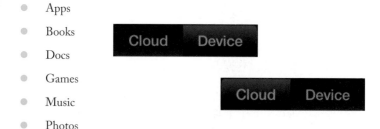

For each item, tap on the **Cloud** or **Device** buttons at the top of the window to view items in the respective areas. When some items are opened in the Cloud they are downloaded automatically to the Device, while others, such as photos, have to be downloaded manually.

For details about downloading and listening to music on your Kindle Fire, see Chapter Five.

Inspiring with apps

Apps are now everywhere in the computing world, particularly in the mobile environment. The Kindle Fire uses some pre-installed Amazon apps and there are thousands more that can be downloaded from the Amazon Appstore. This chapter looks at working with the apps that are already on the Kindle Fire and shows how to find and download more apps so that you can expand your horizons in all directions.

About Kindle Fire apps

Kindle Fire apps are the programs that provide its functionality, whether it is surfing the Web, using email or playing games.

Some apps are pre-installed on the Kindle Fire and these include:

- **Calendar.** This can be used to store information about events, and links to any calendars you have with online webmail accounts
- **Contacts.** This is the Kindle Fire address book that can be used to store contacts' details such as name, email and phone number
- **E-mail.** This app can be used to link to webmail accounts such as GMail, Hotmail or Yahoo!. You can also use it to link to an IMAP or a POP3 email account
- **IMDb.** This is an app that links to a large database of information about movies, TV shows, video games and related information
- **OfficeSuite.** This is a productivity app that can be used to view and edit your documents that have been copied to the Docs library
- **Personal Videos.** This can be used to view your own videos that have been downloaded to your Kindle Fire via your computer
- **Silk.** This is the Kindle Fire web browser
- **Shop Amazon.** This links to the Amazon Shop where you can download a huge range of content

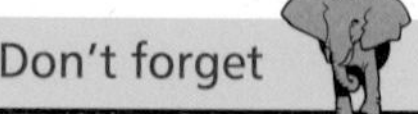

The pre-installed Kindle Fire apps cannot be deleted, but downloaded apps can be.

To view the pre-installed apps:

1. Tap on the **Apps** button on the main Navigation Bar

2. Tap on the **Device** button to view the apps on your Kindle Fire

3. Tap on the **Cloud** button to view some of the apps that are available for your Kindle Fire. The ones with a tick next to them are installed on the device: the ones without a tick are available in the Cloud for downloading. This usually means they have been installed and then deleted from the device

Finding apps

The pre-installed Kindle Fire apps are a good starting point, but you will soon want to start expanding your app horizons. This is done through the Amazon Appstore. To start using this:

1. Tap on the **Apps** button on the main Navigation Bar

   Apps

2. Tap on the **Store** button

   Store >

3. The top panel displays the free apps of the day. Swipe left and right to view more of these

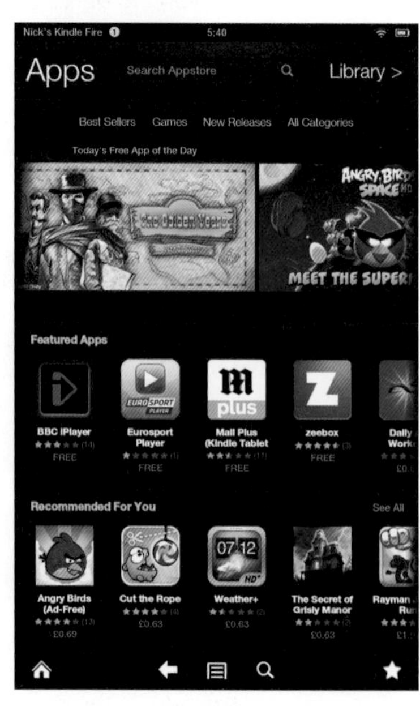

4. The middle panel displays featured apps. Swipe left and right to view more of these

5. The bottom panel has recommendations from Amazon, which are based on your previous purchases (this is only visible in portrait mode)

Searching for apps

There are several options for searching for apps in the Appstore:

1. Tap on these buttons at the top of the Home page window to view apps in different categories

Best Sellers Games New Releases All Categories

2. Tap on the **All Categories** button to view all of the different options

3. Tap on a category to view the apps within it. Within a category, tap on the **All Categories** button (if there is one) to view apps for the main category's sub-categories

4. Tap on the **Refine** button to view apps for specific criteria

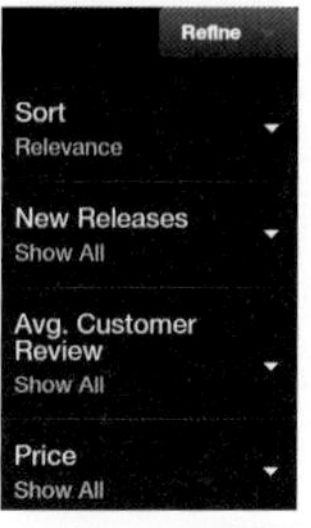

5. Tap in the **Search** box and enter keywords to search the Appstore

Downloading apps

When you find an app that you want to use on your Kindle Fire it can be downloaded in a couple of taps, providing that you have a Wi-Fi connection to the Internet. To do this:

1. Tap on an app to view additional details about it

2. Tap on this button to download the app (if it is a paid-for app it will display the price)

3. Tap on the **Get App** button

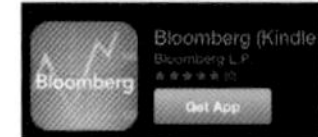

4. As the app is downloading, this is indicated next to the app's icon

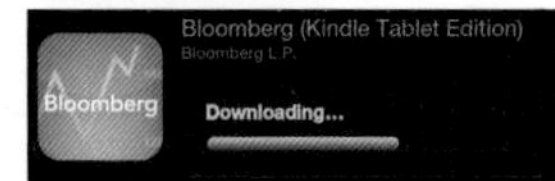

5. Once the app has been downloaded it is available in the Apps library under the **Device** button. Tap on it to open it and start using it

Deleting apps

Apps that have been downloaded can be deleted from your Kindle Fire, in which case they still remain in the Cloud.

1. In the Apps library, tap on the **Device** button

2. Tap and hold on an app that has previously been downloaded

3. Tap on the **Remove from Device** button to delete the app

4. Tap on the **Cloud** button.
The deleted app is still available here.
Tap on it once to reinstall it, or

5. Tap and hold on the app and tap on the **Delete from Cloud** button to remove it completely. If this is done, the app can still be reinstalled from the Appstore. An app can only be removed from the Cloud if it has first been removed from the Device

Apps Settings

Within the Kindle Fire Settings there are a number of options for working with and managing your apps.

1. Swipe down from the top of the screen to access the Status Bar and tap on the **More** button

2. Under the **Settings** heading, tap on the **Applications** link

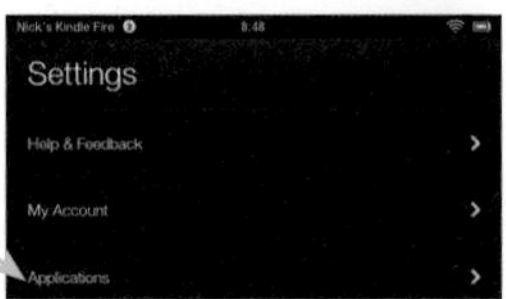

3. The Applications section has a number of options including: notification settings for when apps need to display updated information, details about installed apps (see next page), syncing your Kindle Fire content with your Amazon Cloud content and information relating to the pre-installed Amazon apps such as those for reading audiobooks and playing music

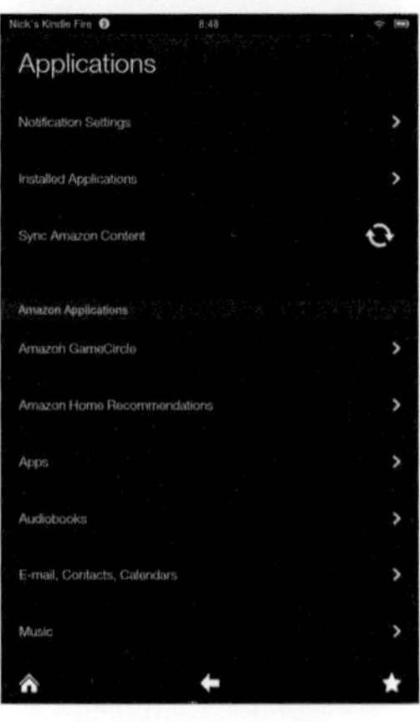

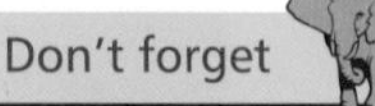

The **E-mail, Contacts, Calendars** link in Step 3 is where you can set up new email accounts.

4 Tap on the **Installed Applications** link in Step 3 to view detailed information about all of the apps on your Kindle Fire. These are not just the apps that appear in the Apps library but all of those on the device

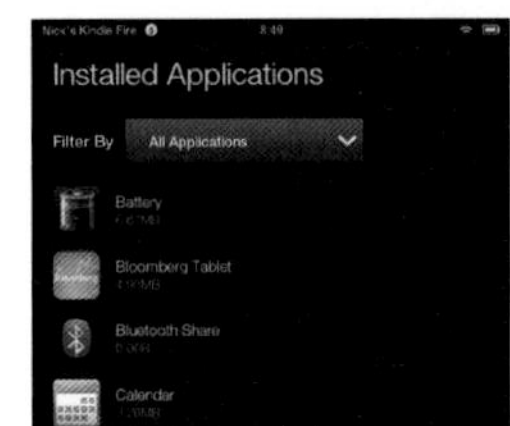

5 Tap on an app to view its full details including how much space it is taking up and the permissions that the app has for accessing other items. Tap on the **Force Stop** button if the app has frozen or stopped working

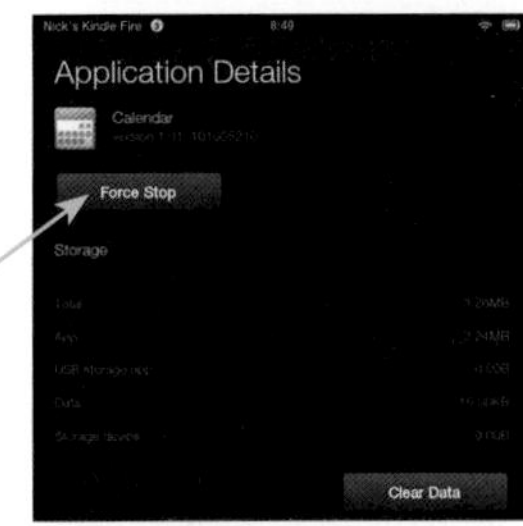

6 If it is an app that has been downloaded from the Appstore, tap on the **Uninstall** button to remove it from your Kindle Fire

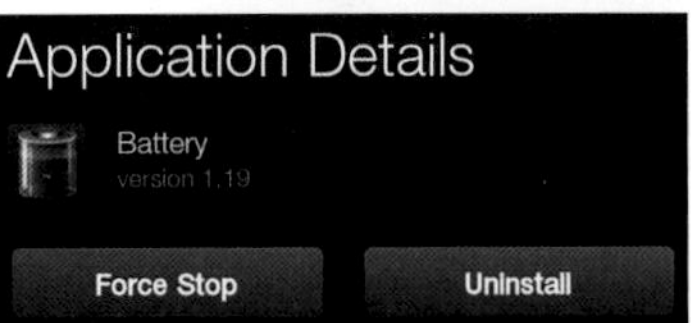

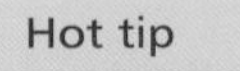

Hot tip

Tap on the **Amazon Home Recommendations** link in Step 3 and tap on the **Hide** button to stop recommendations appearing under the Carousel in portrait mode.

Must-have apps

Everyone has their own ideas about which apps are essential to them, depending on their interests and priorities. However, these are some apps that may be of interest:

- **Angry Birds.** The bestselling Internet game, now available in a Kindle Fire version
- **Calculator Plus Free.** A simple but functional calculator
- **Drawing Pad.** A drawing app for creating your own artwork
- **Evernote.** A useful note-taking app that can be synchronized with versions on other devices too
- **Fruit Ninja.** A simple, but fun, game that consists of slicing different types of fruit with a sword
- **HD Battery.** This is an app that can be used to monitor the battery usage of your Kindle Fire and view how long you can use it for different functions
- **HD Camera.** Use this app to unlock the Kindle Fire's camera. Without the HD Camera app it can only be used for Skype video calls. However, since there is only a front-facing camera this limits its usefulness
- **Pulse**. A news site that collates information from around the Web
- **Smart Writing.** An app for creating text with your own handwriting
- **Temple Run.** A popular game that involves running through a ruined temple, avoiding various obstacles
- **TuneIn Radio.** Use this to listen to the radio on your Kindle Fire

5 Lighting up entertainment

The Kindle Fire is a great device for providing digital entertainment and this chapter looks at using music and video. It details how to download music to your Kindle Fire using the Cloud Player and the Music Importer and then shows how to use it once it is there. The issues around using video on the Kindle Fire are also covered, as is sharing photos via email.

Launching the Cloud Player

Playing music is one of the most popular activities on a tablet and the Kindle Fire provides this functionality with the Music library for storing and playing music. It also links to the Cloud Player for uploading music from your own computer to the Cloud Drive, from where it is then made available to your Kindle Fire. To use the Cloud Player:

1. Access your Cloud Drive in your Amazon Account on the Amazon website (as shown in Chapter Three)

2. At the top of the window, click on the **Launch Cloud Player** link

3. The Cloud Player has a similar interface to the Cloud Drive. Click on one of the **Import your music** buttons

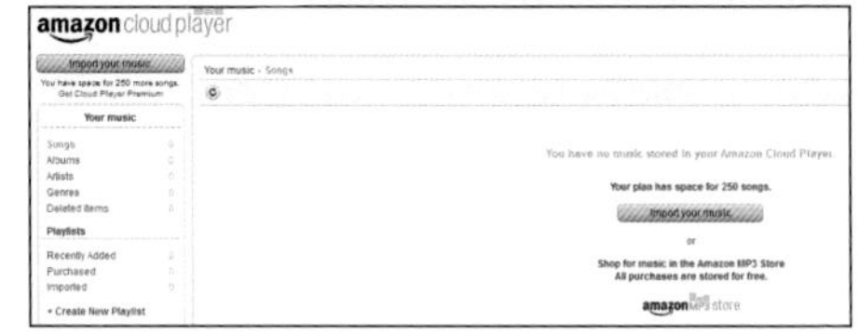

4. You will be prompted to download the Amazon Music Importer. This is used to upload your music to your Cloud Player. Click on the **Download Now** button and follow the installation instructions

Uploading music

The Amazon Music Importer can be used to upload music from your computer, either automatically by scanning your iTunes, Windows Media Player or Music folders, or you can select files manually. To upload music to the Cloud Player using the Music Importer:

1. Click on the **Import your music** button as in Step 3 on the previous page, or click on this button in your computer's programs

2. The Music Importer window has options for scanning your computer or browsing for files

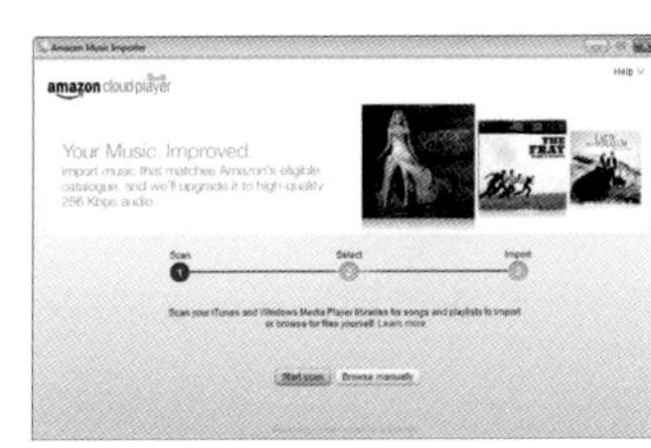

3. Click on the **Browse manually** button

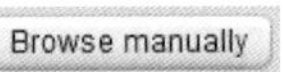

4. Browse to the music files that you want to import and click on the **OK** button

...cont'd

5. To find music automatically with the Music Importer, click on the **Start scan** button

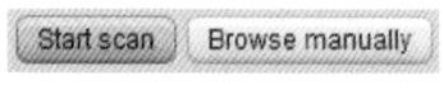

6. The Music Importer will scan over your music content and indicate compatible files for uploading. Click on the **Import all** button

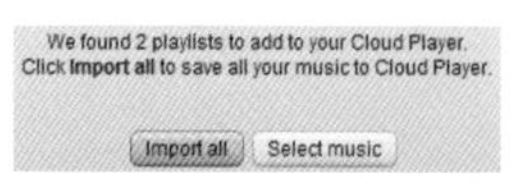

7. The music is added to the Cloud Player (you can upload 250 songs for free to the Cloud Player)

8. Click here to view your music by specific criteria

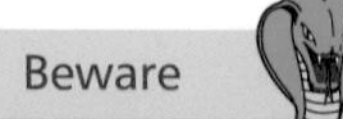

The Amazon Music Importer does not support DRM (Digital Rights Management) AAC files, which are often used in iTunes. These files will have to be converted into another format, for example, MP3, before they are uploaded by the Music Importer.

Transferring music

Music in the Cloud Player can be played on your computer but it can also be downloaded to your Kindle Fire so that you can take it with you wherever you are. To do this:

1. Tap on the **Music** button on the main Navigation Bar

2. Tap on the **Cloud** button. This displays the items that have been uploaded to your Cloud Player

3. Tap on an item to view it. Songs can be played directly from the Cloud, but this requires a Wi-Fi Internet connection

4. Tap on the **Download All** button to download all of the songs in a specific album, or

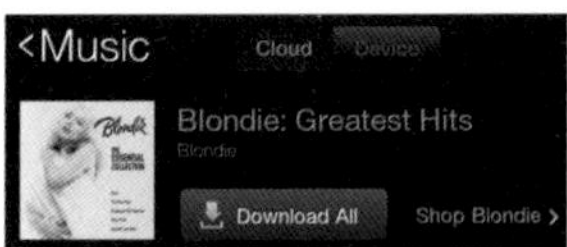

5. Tap and hold on a song and tap on the **Download** button to download it to your Kindle Fire

Managing your music

Once music has been downloaded to your Kindle Fire you can start to organise, and play, your audio collection.

1. Tap on the **Music** button on the main Navigation Bar

2. Tap on the **Device** button to view the items in your Music library

Device

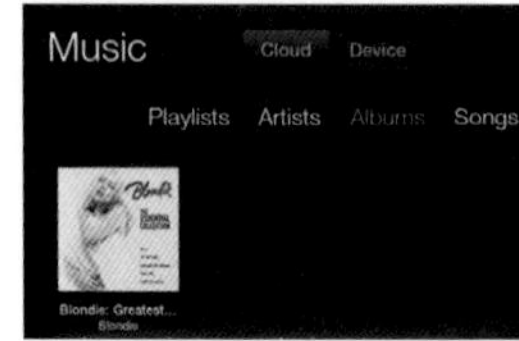

3. Tap on these buttons to view your music collection according to these headings

4. Tap on the **Menu** button on the Options Bar to change the view from list to grid. Tap on the **Downloads** button to view all of the downloaded items

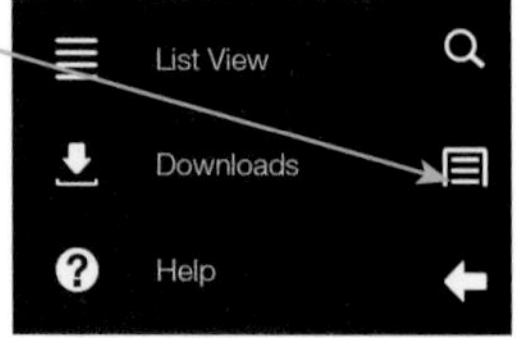

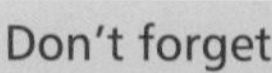

Music can also be bought and downloaded to your Kindle Fire from the Amazon MP3 Store.

Creating a playlist

Within the Music library it is also possible to create playlists, i.e. collections of your favorite songs for specific purposes, such as creating a playlist for a party. To do this:

1. Tap on the **Playlists** button on the Music library navigation bar

2. Tap on **Create New Playlist** button

3. Enter a name for the playlist and tap on the **Save** button

4. Tap on the plus sign button next to a song to add it to the playlist (it will change to a gray button with a minus sign). Tap on the **Done** button to finish adding songs

5. Tap on the **Playlists** button to view available playlists. Tap on a playlist's name to play it. Tap on the **Edit** button to add or delete songs

Playing music

Within the Music library there are a number of options for playing music on your Kindle Fire.

1. Tap on an item in the Music library (if it is an album it will display all of its songs)

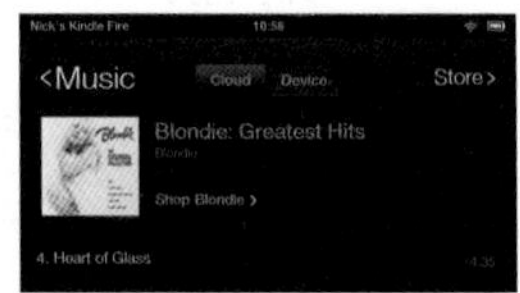

2. Tap on a song to play it in the Music Player

3. Use these buttons to, from left to right, go to the start of the song, play/pause the song, go to the end of the song

4. Drag this slider to increase or decrease the volume

5. Tap on this button so it turns orange to **Shuffle** the order in which songs are played

6. Tap on this button so it turns orange to play the current song, or album, on **Repeat**

7 Tap on the **Hide** button to minimize the Music Player at the bottom of the Music library window. Tap on it to expand it to full size

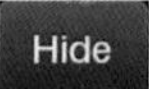

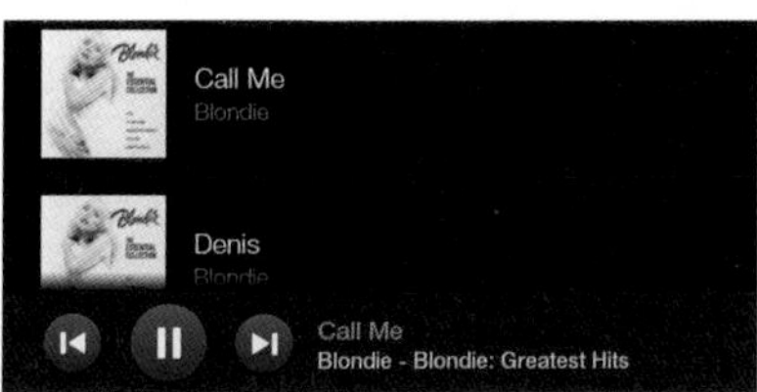

8 Tap on the **Menu** button on the Options Bar and tap on the **Clear Player** button to stop the current song and remove it from the Music Player

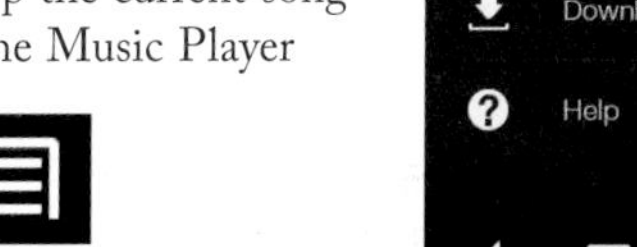

9 When a song is being played you can leave the Music Player and view other areas on your Kindle Fire and the song will continue. It will also be displayed in the **Notifications** area. To see this, swipe down from the top of the screen. The currently-playing song is displayed, along with the playback controls

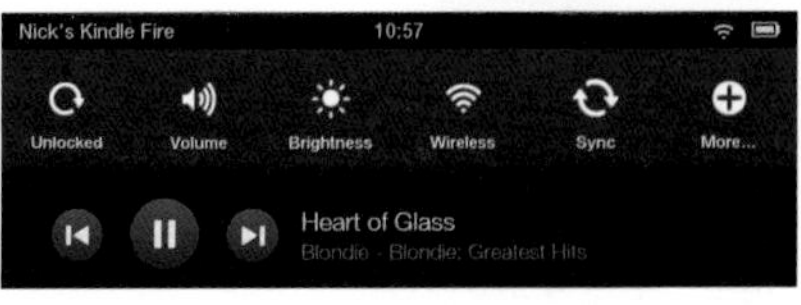

Viewing your own videos

There are two main options for viewing videos on your Kindle Fire:

- Download your videos from your computer, or a removable drive
- View movies and TV shows

To view your own videos:

1. Copy the video to your computer or insert a memory card with the video on it (this should be in MP4 format)

2. Connect your Kindle Fire with the Micro-B/USB Connector cable. Open the Kindle Fire's **Internal storage**

3. Navigate to the **Movies** folder in your Kindle Fire's file structure. Double-click on it to open it

4. Copy the video file into the **Movies** folder. Other videos can be copied here too but if they are in an incompatible format, e.g. Windows Media Video (WMV) they will not be visible on your Kindle Fire

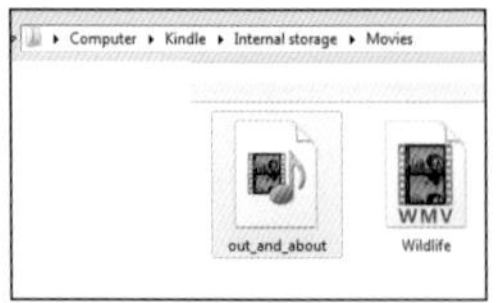

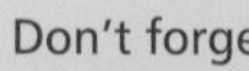

Don't forget

Compatible video formats on the Kindle Fire are MP4 or VP8.

5. Tap on the **Apps** button on your Kindle Fire's main Navigation Bar

6. Tap on the **Personal Videos** app

7. Compatible videos will be displayed in the app

8. Tap and hold on a video to access options for deleting it (**Delete** button) and viewing file information about it (**Item Details** button)

9. Tap on a video to play it in the Video Player

Viewing movies and more

If you want to download and watch commercial movies and TV shows this can be done through a subscription service provided by Amazon for this type of content.

1. Tap on the **Videos** button on the main Navigation Bar

2. Depending on your location, you are offered the appropriate download service. In the US this can be done through the Amazon Prime service, or with an appropriate app such as Netflix, while in the UK it is done through the Amazon company LOVEFiLM. (Both services offer a 30-day trial). For other geographic locations there may not be a video download service for the Kindle Fire

Using Amazon Prime and Amazon Instant Video

In the US, the Amazon Prime service can be used to stream and also download movies and TV shows. This cost US $79/year *(correct at the time of printing)* and the Kindle Fire has to be located in the US and the user has to have a US credit card. This also provides access to Amazon Instant Video which can be used to rent or buy video content so that it can be downloaded and viewed offline (each item must be paid for in addition to the Amazon Prime subscription).

Using LOVEFiLM

In the UK, LOVEFiLM can be used to stream video content:

1. Tap on an item to view its details. Tap on the **Watch Now** button to start viewing

Issues with video

Although you can watch a wide range of video content on your Kindle Fire there are still some issues associated with this:

- When watching movies or TV shows from Prime, Instant or LOVEFiLM the content is streamed to your Kindle Fire. This means that it is sent to your Kindle Fire as you are watching it over a Wi-Fi connection. The advantage of this is that it is a more efficient use of the bandwidth of the Wi-Fi, but the disadvantage is that you have to be in range of a Wi-Fi connection in order to watch the content. With Amazon Instant Video in the US, movies and TV shows can also be downloaded to your Kindle Fire, but in the UK they can only be streamed, so you cannot watch them offline *(correct at the time of printing)*
- Since the Kindle Fire supports a limited number of video file formats (MP4 and VP8) a lot of video files will not play on your Kindle Fire. This could include your own home videos and also any commercial movies that you have copied to your computer. One option for overcoming this is to use a video encoder to convert your videos into a Kindle Fire compatible format (MP4 is the best option). These are programs that convert one video file format into your selected one. There are dozens of programs available on the Web, for Windows and Mac. Some are free, while others have to be paid for. Enter 'video encoders' into a web search engine to find a list of options
- The Kindle Fire web browser, Silk, does not support Flash, so it will not play Flash video content on the Web. However, this is becoming less of an issue than it would have been a few years ago, as fewer websites are relying on Flash. But it is still a consideration to bear in mind if you need to use Flash

Sharing photos

As shown in Chapter Three, photos can be uploaded to your Cloud Drive on the Amazon website and then downloaded to your Kindle Fire. They can also be copied into the **Pictures** folder in the file structure by connecting the Kindle Fire to your computer with the Micro-B/USB Connector (in the same way as copying videos as shown on page 60). Whatever way that you obtain photos, they can be viewed through the Photos app and emailed to other people. To do this:

1. Tap on the **Photos** button on the main Navigation Bar

Photos

2. In either the **Cloud** or **Device** section, open a photo. Tap on the **Menu** button on the Options Bar and tap on the **Send** button

3. Tap on the **E-mail** button to attach the photo to a blank email, or

4. Select multiple photos by tapping on them and tap on this button to attach them directly to a new email

6 Igniting a passion for reading

The original Kindle was developed as an eReader for ebooks, magazines and newspapers. The Kindle Fire has continued this tradition and reading is still one of its major uses. This chapter looks at obtaining books for your Kindle Fire and how to navigate your way around them and share your own thoughts and opinions with the online Kindle book community.

Obtaining books

Amazon started life as an online bookseller and there is an unsurpassed range of content for the Kindle Fire here. Books are stored and accessed from the Books library, from where you can also access the full range of Kindle books on the Amazon website. (Magazines and newspapers can be accessed in a similar way, using the **Newsstand** button.)

1. Tap on the **Books** button on the main Navigation Bar

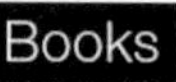

2. Tap on the **Device** button to view the books that you already have on your Kindle Fire

3. Tap on the **Cloud** button to view all of the books that you have downloaded, including those downloaded on other devices. The ones that have already been downloaded to your Kindle Fire are denoted with a tick

There are two dictionaries that are pre-loaded onto the Kindle Fire, which appear in the **Device** Book library.

4 Tap on a title in the **Cloud** to download it to your Kindle Fire, where it appears under the **Device** button with a **New** tag on it

5 Tap on the **Store** button to go to the online Amazon Kindle Store

6 Navigate through the Store using the main panels, or

7 Tap under the **Categories** heading to view books in these specific categories

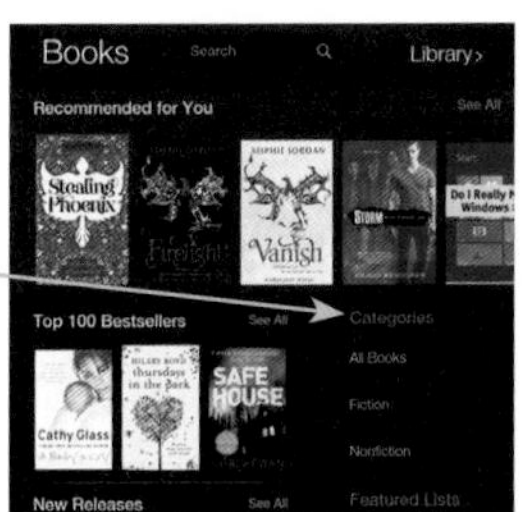

8 Tap on a title to view more details about it, including a description and customer reviews

9 Tap on this button to buy a book. This will be downloaded to your Kindle Fire and also be available in the Cloud

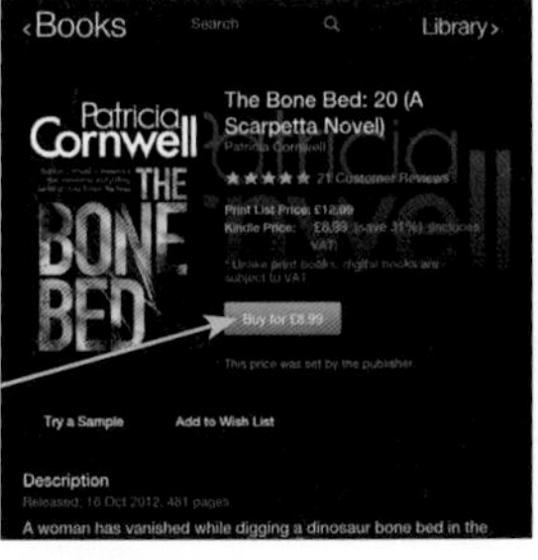

Book Settings

With hard copy books there is very little flexibility in terms of changing the type of paper or the size of the text. However, with a Kindle book you have a range of settings that you can change and customize.

1. Open a book and tap in the middle of a page
2. Tap on the **Settings** button
3. Tap on one of the **Font Size** buttons to make the text larger or smaller
4. Tap on one of the **Color Mode** buttons to use black text on a white background, a sepia background, or white text on a black background

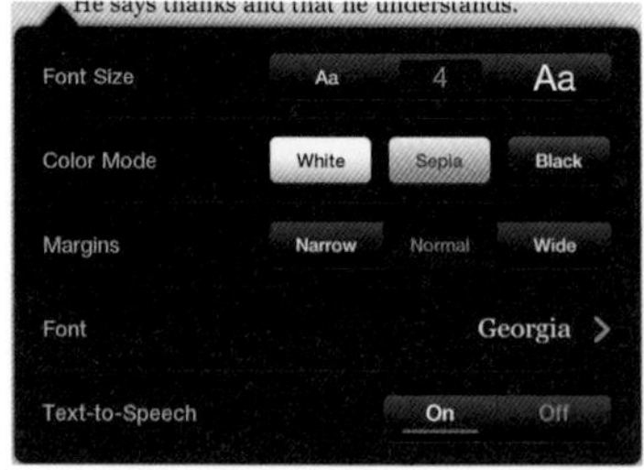

5. Tap on one of the **Margins** buttons to specify how much space appears around the text
6. Tap on the **Font** link to change the font used in the book. There are six other options from which to choose

Reading aloud

The final option in the Settings section is for the Text-to-Speech function with Kindle books. If this is enabled, books with this functionality can be read aloud by your Kindle Fire. To do this:

1. Access the Settings section as on the previous page

2. Tap on the **On** button next to **Text-to-Speech**

3. Tap in the middle of a page to access the bottom Location Bar. If it has Text-to-Speech functionality this is denoted by a **Play** button at the left-hand side of the Location Bar

4. Tap on the **Play** button to start the Kindle Fire reading the book. This is done with a computer-generated voice and so is more monotone than if it were being read by an actual person

If you tap too close to the edge of the page to access the Settings or Location Bar you may turn the page instead. Make sure you tap in the middle of the page to avoid this.

Thumbing through books

A common concern with ebooks is that you will lose your place and not be able to find it again. However, Kindle books have great flexibility for navigating around so that you can quickly move to specific points in your book including pages and locations.

1. Open a book and tap in the middle of a page

2. Tap on the **Go To** button

3. Swipe up and down to access specific chapters

4. Tap on this button to go to the furthest point that you have got to in the book. This is useful if you also read the book on another device

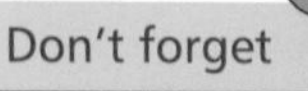

The Location Bar at the bottom of the screen displays the location and page numbers. The location numbers are specific to individual lines of text to make it easier to locate items.

5. Tap on this button to go to a specific location

Go to Page or Location

6. Enter the location or page number and tap on the appropriate button

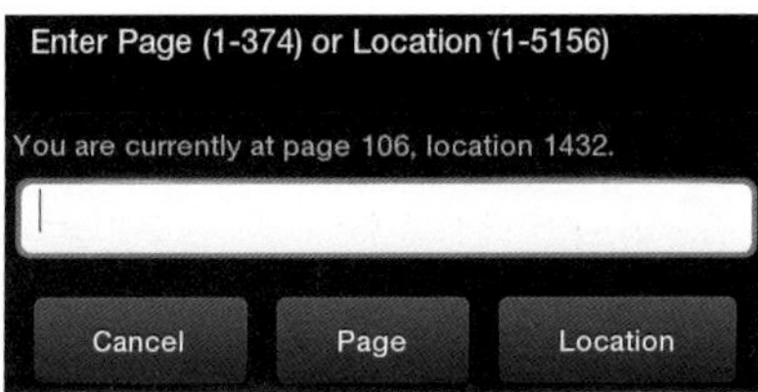

7. Not all Kindle books have page numbers attached to them. For those that do, this is indicated in their **Product Details** in the Kindle Bookstore. If there is a **Page # Source ISBN** this means that the Kindle book has page numbers that correspond to the hard copy

Product Details

Sales Rank: #92 Paid in Kindle Store
Language: English
Print Length: 384 pages
Page # Source ISBN: 1846551455

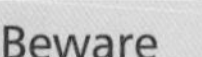

Unlike the original Kindle, the Kindle Fire has a LCD screen which means that it is backlit and makes it brighter for reading. Some people prefer this, while others prefer the original screen.

Adding Notes and Bookmarks

If you like taking notes while you are reading books you no longer have to worry about jotting down your thoughts in the margins or on pieces of paper. With Kindle books you can add your own electronic notes and also insert bookmarks at your favorite passages. To do this:

1. Tap and hold to activate the magnifier icon and drag it over text to highlight it

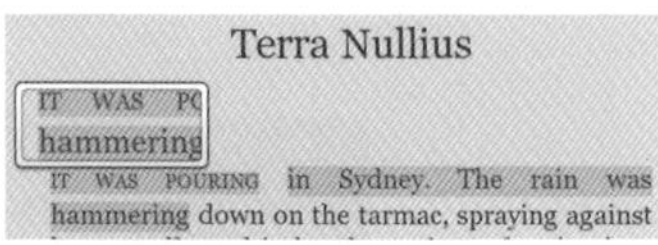

2. Tap on the **Note** button (tap on the **Highlight** button to add a yellow highlight)

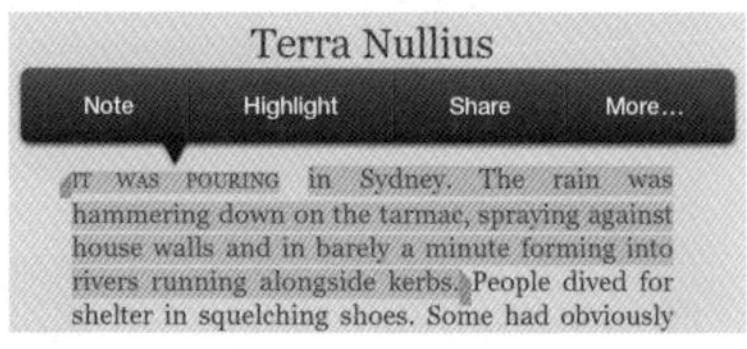

3. Enter the note that applies to the selected text and tap on the **Save** button

4. A note is indicated by a small blue icon next to the highlighted text. Tap on this to view details of the note

5 To view all of your notes, tap in the middle of a page and tap on the **Notes** button

6 Notes and highlighted text are shown on the **My Notes & Marks** page. Tap on an item to go to that point in the book

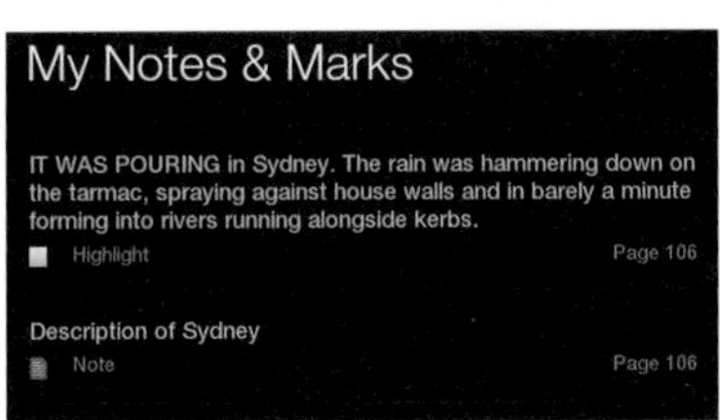

Adding bookmarks

1 To bookmark a page in a book, tap in the top right-hand corner. Tap again to remove it

2 Bookmarks are included on the **My Notes & Marks** page. Tap on a bookmark to go to that location

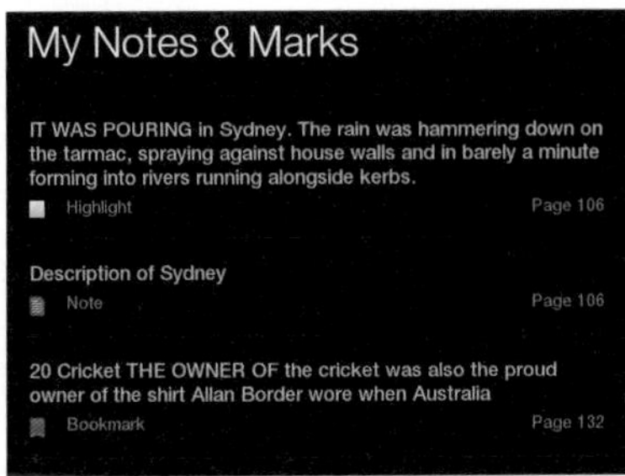

Sharing your thoughts

Reading Kindle books can be a very collaborative experience: you can easily share passages and your thoughts and opinions with the online Kindle community and see what other people have to say about the books they are reading.

1. Highlight a piece of text and tap on the **Share** button

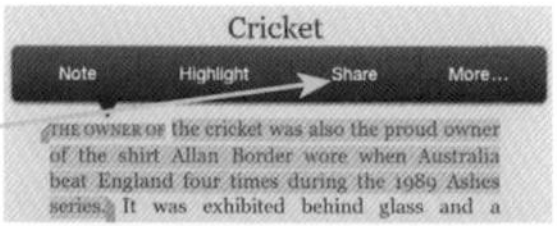

2. Enter any comments and tap on the **Share** button. If you do not add any comments, just the highlighted text will be shared

3. Enter a name that will appear next to the item and tap on the **Register and Share** button

4. The text and comments appear in the Share section

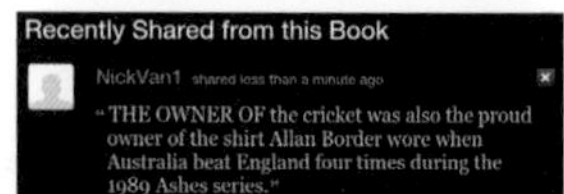

5. To delete a shared item, tap on the cross next to it and tap on the **Delete** button

Finding Definitions

One of the great things about reading is that we not only get a lot of enjoyment from it, but also learn new things. Kindle books are excellent for expanding our vocabularies, without having to resort to looking up a separate dictionary. This is done with the definition feature:

1. Tap and hold on a word to see a quick definition about it

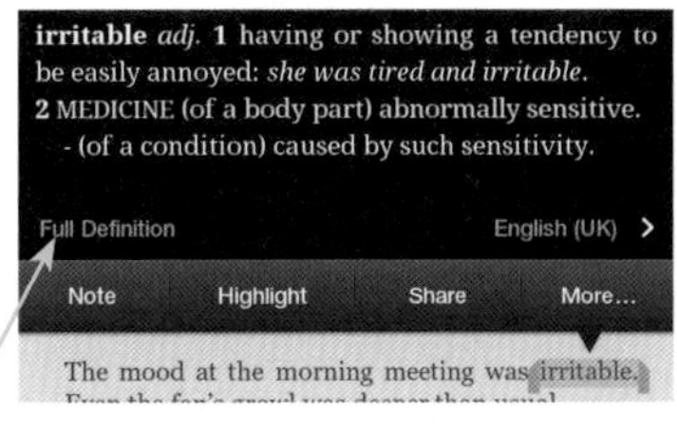

irritable *adj.* 1 having or showing a tendency to be easily annoyed: *she was tired and irritable.*
2 MEDICINE (of a body part) abnormally sensitive.
- (of a condition) caused by such sensitivity.
Full Definition
English (UK) >
Note
Highlight
Share
More...
The mood at the morning meeting was irritable.

2. Tap on the **Full Definition** link in Step 1 to see a more extensive explanation of the word (tap on the **English** link to select a dictionary language)

irritable *adj.* 1 having or showing a tendency to be easily annoyed: *she was tired and irritable.*
2 MEDICINE (of a body part) abnormally sensitive.
- (of a condition) caused by such sensitivity.
- [BIOLOGY] (of a living organism) having the property of responding actively to physical stimuli.

<DERIVATIVES> irritably *adv.*
<ORIGIN> mid 17th century: from Latin ***irritabilis***, from the verb ***irritare*** (see IRRITATE).

3. Tap on the **More** button in Step 1 to search for the selected word throughout the book, in Wikipedia or on the Web

Search in Book
Search Wikipedia
Search the Web

Turning on the X-Ray

The X-Ray feature for books on the Kindle Fire can be used to view the 'bare bones' of a page, chapter or book. This highlights characters, locations or terms, provides additional information about them, if applicable, and shows where they occur at specific locations.

1. Tap in the middle of a page and tap on the **X-Ray** button

2. The people, places and terms are listed on the X-Ray page. The more blue lines next to an item, the more entries it has. (If a book supports the X-Ray function this will be noted under its Product Details on Amazon)

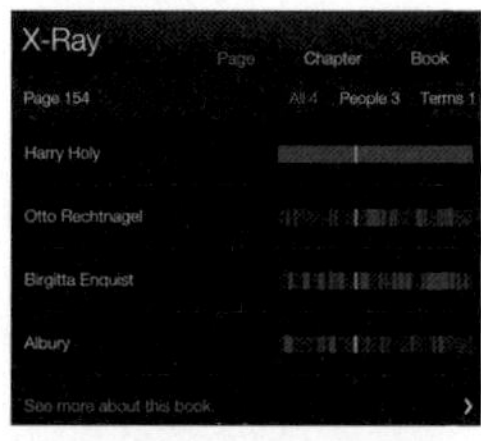

3. Tap on an entry to see fuller details about it and examples of where it appears on the page, in the chapter or in the book

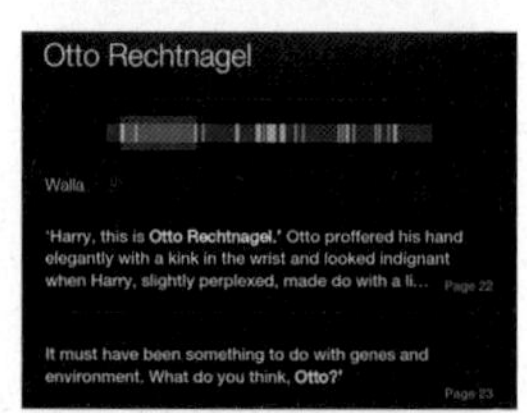

4. Drag the slider on the top bar to move through all of the entries for the selected item

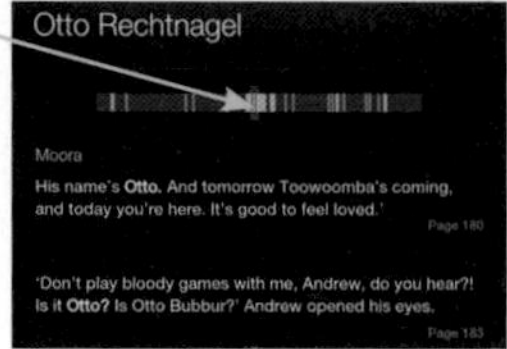

Bringing the Web to life

On the Kindle Fire the Web is accessed through the Silk browser. This chapter introduces using Silk and covers popular browsing issues such as using tabs, navigating around the Web, bookmarking pages and working with links and images. It also details the Settings for the Silk browser so that you can adapt it for your own requirements.

Browsing on the Kindle Fire

Web browsing is an essential part of everyday life and the Kindle Fire provides this with its own web browser, called Silk. This provides a fast, fluid browsing experience with its own interface and settings. To use Silk to access the Web:

1. Tap on the **Web** button on the main Navigation Bar, or

2. Tap on the **Apps** button on the main Navigation Bar and tap on the Silk app

3. Tap and hold on the Silk app and tap on the **Add to Favorites** button

4. Tap on the **Favorites** button on the Options Bar to access the Silk browser at any time

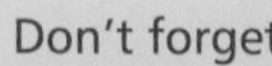

Don't forget

The Silk browser uses cloud data (based on Amazon's vast databases) to speed up page rendering and performance.

Getting Silky

The Silk browser has a slightly different interface to the one that many people may be used to from using desktop and laptop computers, but most of its functionality is similar. To use the Silk browser:

1. Access the Silk browser as shown on the previous page. The first page that appears is the **Starter** page. This contains thumbnail links, a Search/Address box and some navigation buttons. This is also the page that appears when a new tab is opened in the Silk browser

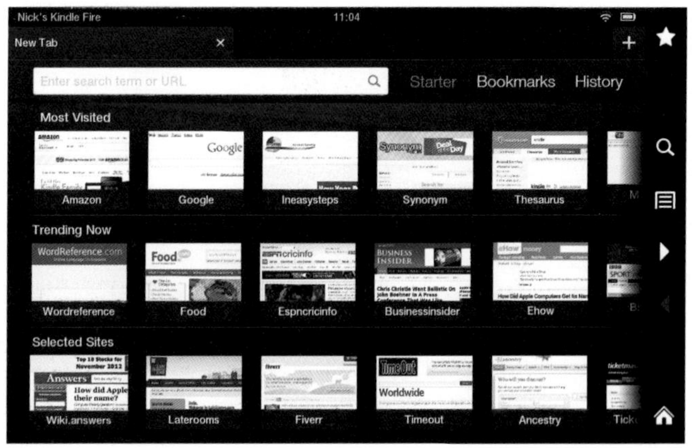

2. Use these buttons to access the **Bookmarks** or **History** pages, or return to the **Starter** page

Starter Bookmarks History

Opening pages

Web pages can be opened directly from the Starter page, either from the thumbnails or by entering a web address or search word into the Search/Address box at the top of the browser.

1. On the Starter page, tap on one of the thumbnails under the **Most Visited**, **Trending Now** or **Selected Sites** sections. These will change as you visit different websites

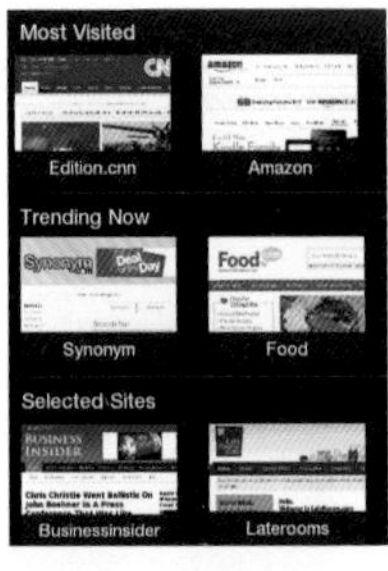

2. Tap in the **Search/ Address** box. Previously-visited pages are shown underneath. Tap on one to go to that page, or

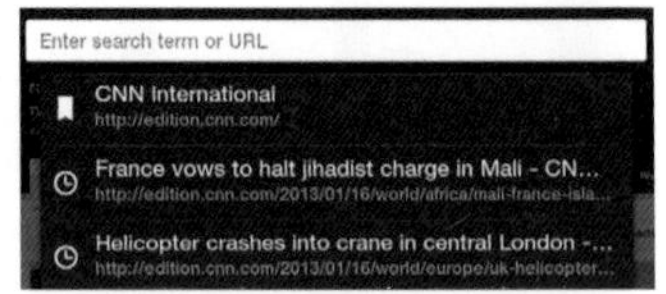

3. Enter a website address or search word into the box. As you type, suggestions will appear. Tap on one to go to a list of search results and tap on one to go to that page

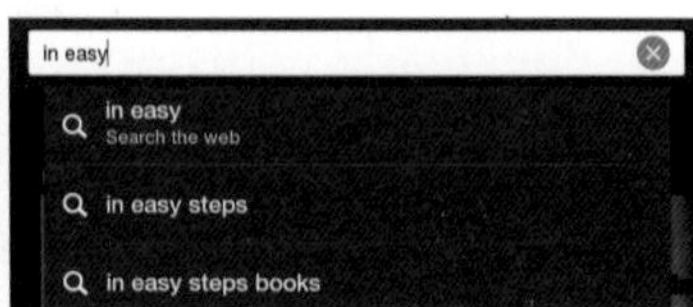

Finding your way around

The navigation in the Silk browser is mostly done through the Kindle Fire's **Options Bar**, which appears along the border of the browser.

1. Tap on the **Menu** button on the Options Bar to access options for returning to the Starter page, sharing a link to the current page via email, finding specific words or phrases on a page, the Silk browser Settings, viewing items you have downloaded and the Silk Help

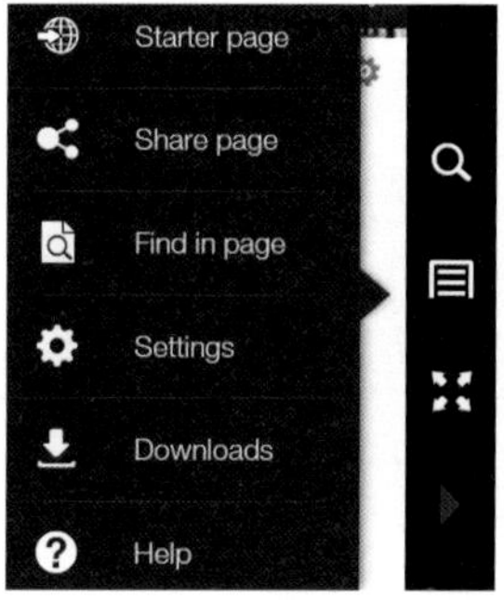

2. Tap on these buttons to move forwards and backwards through pages that you have already visited

3. Tap on this button to view the current web page at full screen. This hides the Options Bar and the Tabs Bar at the top of the screen. Swipe inwards (or upwards) on this button to return to standard view

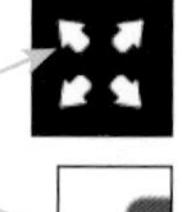

Pinch outwards with thumb and forefinger (or double-tap) on a web page to zoom in on it. Pinch inwards to zoom out again.

Bookmarking pages

The favorite pages that you visit will show up in the **Most Visited** section on the **Starter** page. It is also possible to bookmark pages so that you can find them quickly. To do this:

1. Open the page that you want to bookmark and tap on this button to the left of the Search/Address box

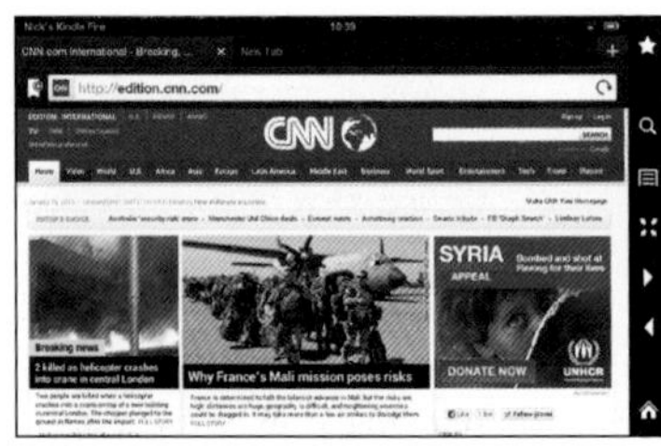

2. Tap in the **Name** box and enter a name for the bookmark. Tap on the **OK** button

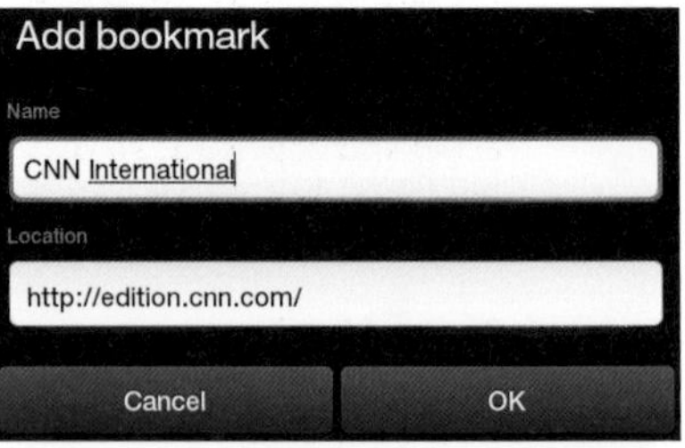

3. To view bookmarks, access the Starter page, as shown in Step 1 on page 81, and tap on the **Bookmarks** link

Links and images

Links and images are both essential items on websites: links provide the functionality for moving between pages and sites, while images provide the all-important graphical element. To work with these:

1. Tap and hold on a link to access its menu (tap once on a link to go directly to the linked page). The options on the menu are for opening the link in the current tab, opening it in a new tab, opening it in a new tab while you remain viewing the current tab (background option), adding the link as a bookmark, sharing it via email and copying it so that it could be pasted into the Search/Address box

2. Tap and hold on an image to access its menu. The options are for saving it (into your Photos library), viewing it on a page on its own, or adding it to an Amazon Wish List to share with other people

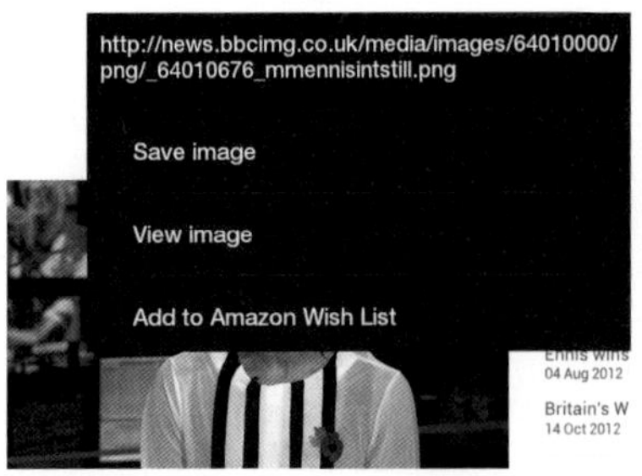

Adding tabs

The Silk browser supports the use of tabs, whereby you can open numerous pages within the same browser window. To do this:

1. Tap on this button at the top right-hand corner of the browser window to add a new tab

2. Open a new page from the Starter page or by entering a web address or search word into the Search/Address box

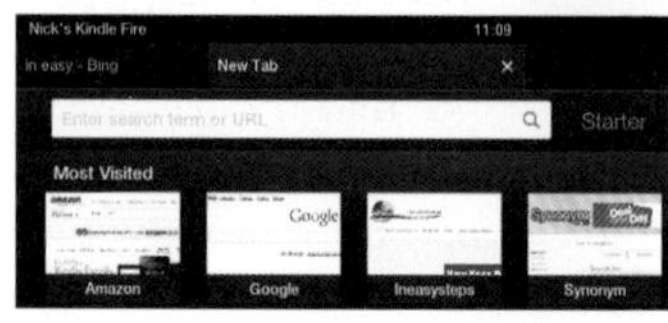

3. New tabs are opened at the top of the browser

4. Tap and hold on a tab name to view the tab menu with options for closing tabs, bookmarking the current page or adding it to favorites

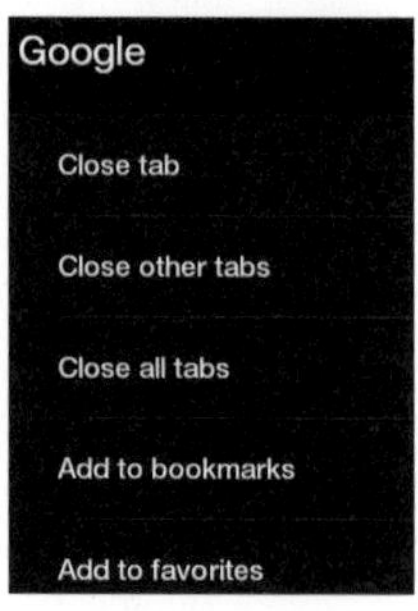

Don't forget

Up to ten tabs can be added in the Silk browser. As more are added, swipe left and right to view all of the available tabs.

History and Reader

History

To view your Silk browsing history:

1. From the Starter page, tap on the **History** button

2. Recently-visited pages are displayed, grouped according to the time and day on which they were viewed

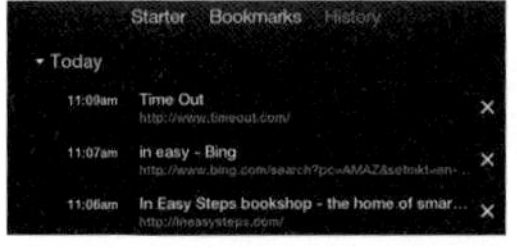

Using the Reader

The Reader function enables you to read web pages with only the text and not any other content.

1. If a web page has this button on its tab it indicates that the Reader function is available. Tap on it to view the page in **Reader** format

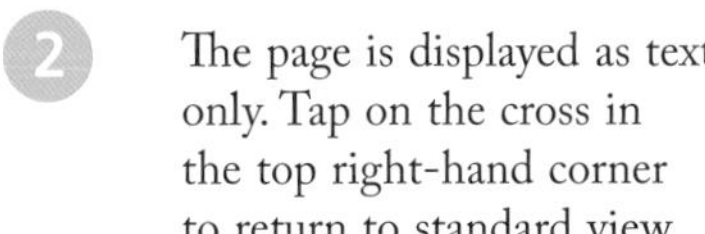

2. The page is displayed as text only. Tap on the cross in the top right-hand corner to return to standard view

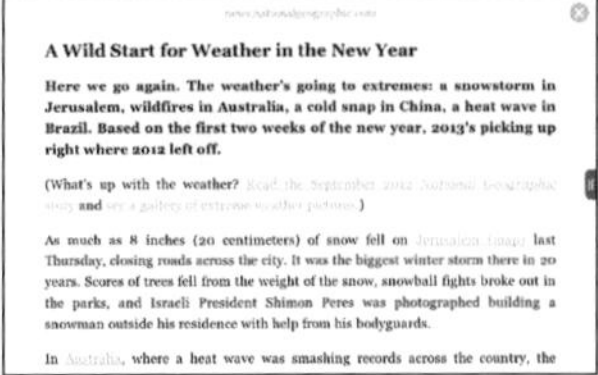

A Wild Start for Weather in the New Year

Here we go again. The weather's going to extremes: a snowstorm in Jerusalem, wildfires in Australia, a cold snap in China, a heat wave in Brazil. Based on the first two weeks of the new year, 2013's picking up right where 2012 left off.

(What's up with the weather? Read the September 2012 National Geographic story and see a gallery of extreme weather pictures.)

As much as 8 inches (20 centimeters) of snow fell on Jerusalem (map) last Thursday, closing roads across the city. It was the biggest winter storm there in 20 years. Scores of trees fell from the weight of the snow, snowball fights broke out in the parks, and Israeli President Shimon Peres was photographed building a snowman outside his residence with help from his bodyguards.

In Australia, where a heat wave was smashing records across the country, the

Silk Settings

For the functional side of using Silk, there are several settings that can be accessed to customise the way that the browser works. This is done from the Settings button:

1. Tap on the **Menu** button and tap on the **Settings** button

2. The available settings are displayed. Tap on one to view its options. Three useful ones are: **Search engine**, where you can select a default search engine for Silk; **Display most recent page in Carousel**, which can be checked on or off to display, or hide, the most recently visited web page in the Carousel; and **Clear history**, which can be used to remove all information from your browsing history

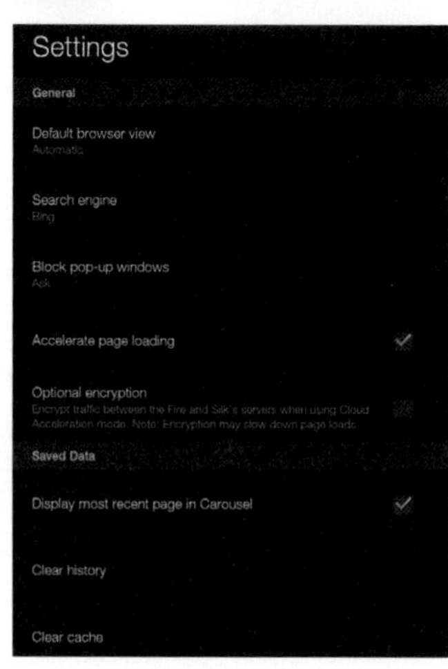

Hot tip

The Search/Address box on the Silk browser is also where you can **Refresh** the web page you are currently viewing. Tap on the icon at the right-hand side of the box to do this.

Keep the flame burning

Keeping in touch with people is an important part of life, and the digital world now gives us even more ways in which to do this. This chapter shows how to use your Kindle Fire to make sure you keep in touch with family, friends and business contacts, using email, address books, calendars, social networking sites and Skype for telephone and video calls.

Adding email accounts

Email functionality on the Kindle Fire is provided by the E-mail app. This is an app that enables you to link to your email accounts (either webmail, IMAP or POP3 accounts) so that you can get all of your emails on your Kindle Fire. To set up email accounts:

1. Tap on the **Apps** link on the main Navigation Bar

2. Tap on the **E-mail** app

3. Tap on the type of account that you want to add

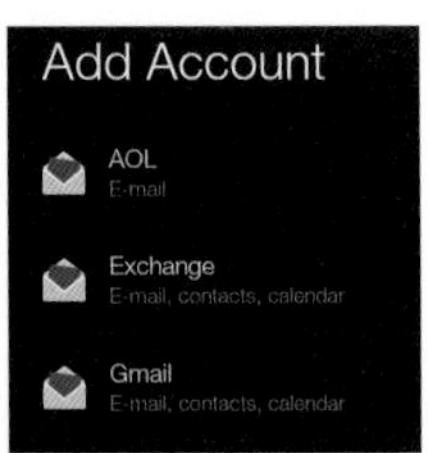

4. Enter the details of your email account and tap on the **Next** button (this should be a webmail account that you have already set up and are using)

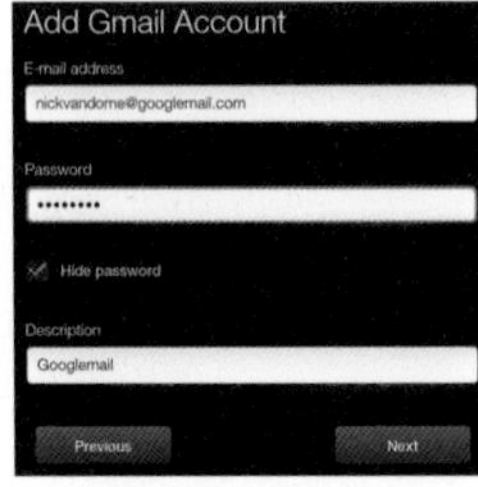

Add the E-mail app to your Favorites so that it is always quickly available for accessing your messages.

5 Tap on the **Save** button to complete the account setup

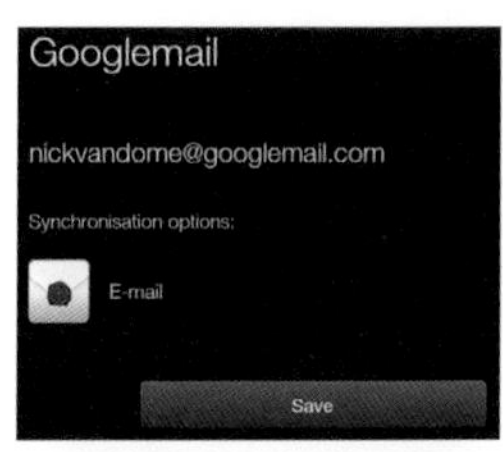

6 Tap on one of the options for viewing the Inbox for the new account, going to its Settings, or adding another account

7 To add an account that is not on the list in Step 3, tap on the **Other Provider** button and enter the account settings

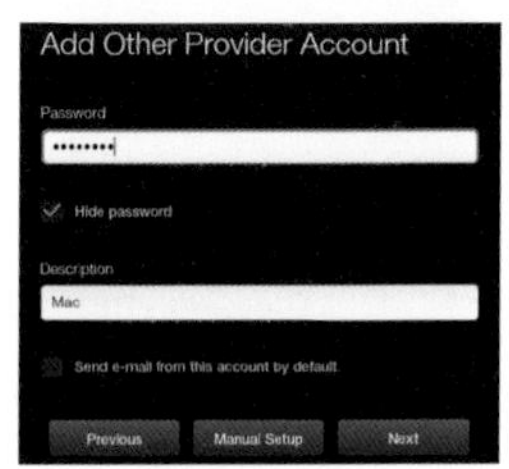

8 If the account is not recognised automatically, tap on the **Manual Setup** button and add the required server settings

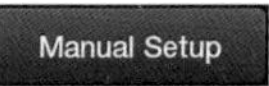

When using Manual Setup you may need to change the **Security Type** and **Require sign-in** options in order for the account to be authorised.

Working with email

Sending an email

Once an email account has been set up, it will be accessed when you tap on the **E-mail** app.

1. The available accounts will be displayed. If more than one account has been added they will all be displayed here

2. Tap on an account to view its **Inbox**. Tap on a message to view it

3. Tap on the **New** button to create a new message and then the **Send** button to send it

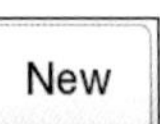

Email settings

Email settings can be accessed for specific accounts and also general email settings that apply to any account. To apply general settings:

1. In the E-mail app, tap on the **Menu** button and tap on the **Settings** link

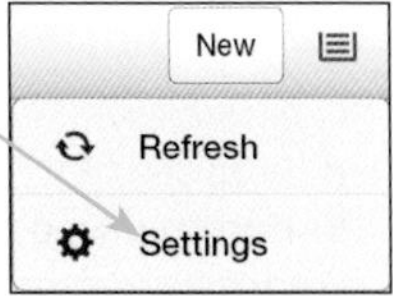

2. Tap on the **E-mail General Settings** button

3. Select options for text size in emails, showing images, downloading attachments automatically and whether to include the original message in a reply

4. Tap on an account name on the page in Step 2 to view its specific settings. These include options for checking for new emails, adding a signature to emails and the account server settings

Deleting an email account

To delete an email account:

1. Access the settings for an account as in Step 4 above and tap on the **Remove Account** button

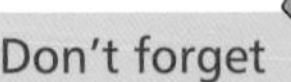

The email Settings can also be accessed by swiping down from the top of the screen and tapping on the **More** button. Then tap on the **Applications** button and the **E-mail, Contacts, Calendars** button.

Adding contacts

An important part of staying in touch with people is having an up-to-date address book. On the Kindle Fire you can use the Contacts app:

1. Tap on the **Apps** link on the main Navigation Bar

2. Tap on the **Contacts** app

3. Tap on the **Set Up My Profile** link

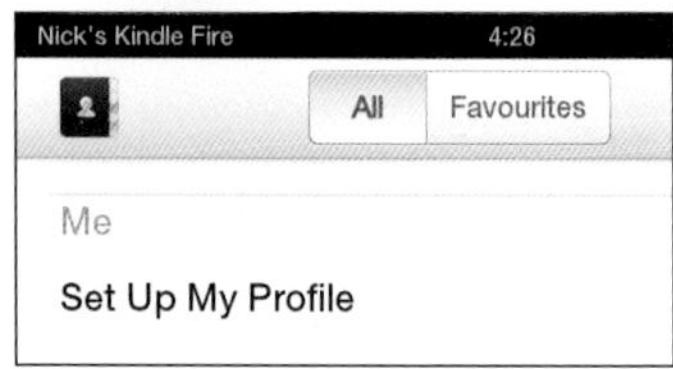

4. Enter your contact details, including name, email and phone number and tap on the **Save** button

Save

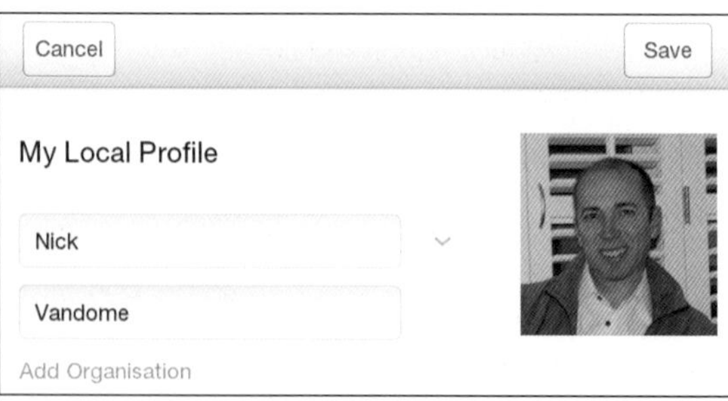

5 Your own profile is added in the Contacts app. Tap on this button to go back to the Contacts app's Home page

6 Tap on the **New** button to add a new contact

7 All contacts are displayed alphabetically on the Contacts app's Home page. Tap on one to view their details

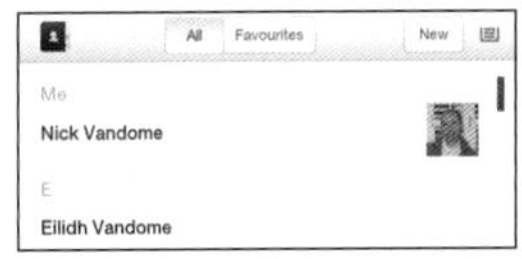

8 Access a contact and tap on this button to add them as a favorite within the Contacts app

9 Tap on the **Menu** button and tap on the **Settings** link to access the E-Mail, Contacts, Calendars Settings

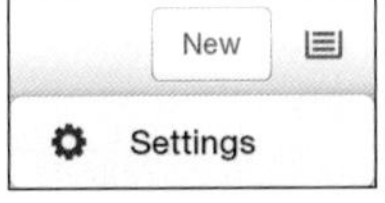

10 Tap on the **Contacts General Settings** button to view these, which include backing up to the Amazon Cloud and sorting options

Using calendars

The Calendar app can be used to link to your online accounts (as with adding an email account) so that you can add events and have them available through your online service and also on your Kindle Fire.

1. Tap on the **Apps** link on the main Navigation Bar

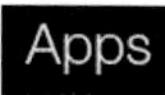

2. Tap on the **Calendar** app

3. The calendar is displayed and the view can be customized in a number of ways

4. Tap on this button to view the current day at any point

5. Tap on these buttons at the top of the window to view the calendar in list view or by day, week or month

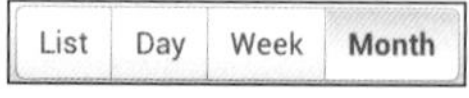

6. Tap on these buttons at the bottom of the window to view specific months. Swipe left and right to view different months

Adding events

To add events to the calendar:

1. In Day or Week View, tap and hold on a time slot and tap on the **New Event** button

3:00pm, Wednesday

New Event

2. You will be prompted to add an online account so that it can synchronize with your Kindle Fire calendar. Once this is done you can enter the time and place for the event and set reminders

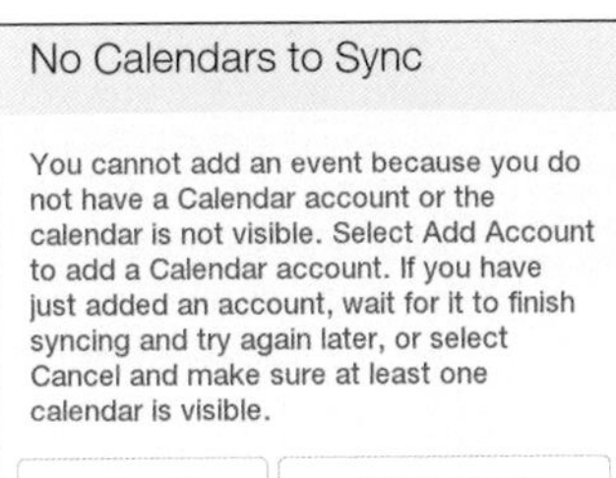

No Calendars to Sync
You cannot add an event because you do not have a Calendar account or the calendar is not visible. Select Add Account to add a Calendar account. If you have just added an account, wait for it to finish syncing and try again later, or select Cancel and make sure at least one calendar is visible.
Cancel
Add Account

Settings

To access the Calendar settings:

1. Tap on the **Menu** button and tap on the **Calendars to Display** link to view available online calendars. Tap on the **Settings** link to access the Calendar Settings

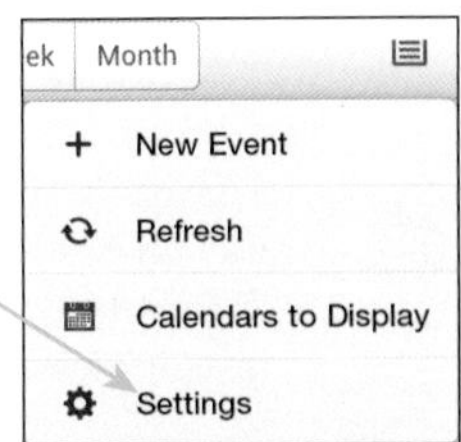

2. Tap on this button to view **Calendar General Settings**

Contacting with Skype

Skype is a useful service that enables you to make voice and video calls to other Skype users, free of charge. To use Skype:

1. Tap on the **Apps** link on the main Navigation Bar

2. Under the **Cloud** button, tap on the **Skype** button. This will download the app to your Kindle Fire (or get it from the Appstore). Tap on it to open it

3. If you already have a Skype account, enter your details, or tap on the **Create an account** button to create a new account

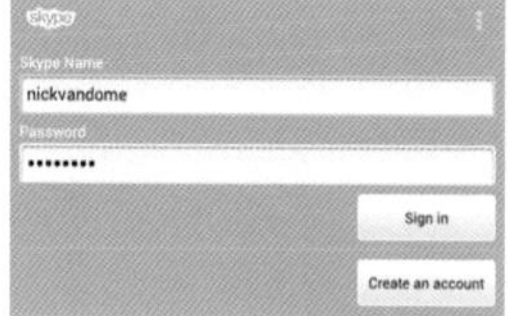

4. Tap on the **Contacts** button to view your current contacts and add new ones

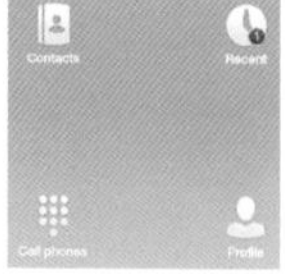

5. Tap on a contact to view their details and contact them by voice, video or instant messaging

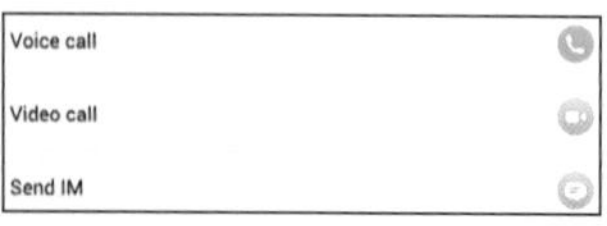

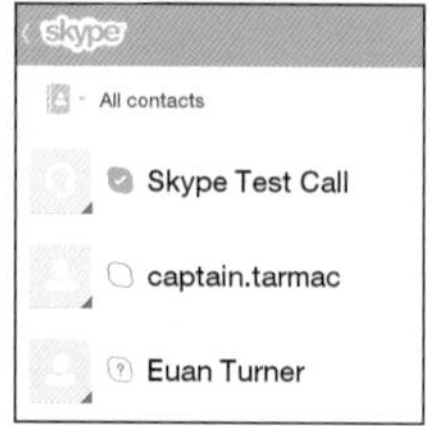

Adding contacts

To add new contacts to call in Skype:

1. Access the **Contacts** section and tap on this button

2. Enter the name you want to search for and tap on the **Search** icon again

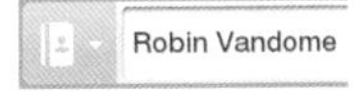

3. Tap on the **Search Skype directory** button to search for the requested person

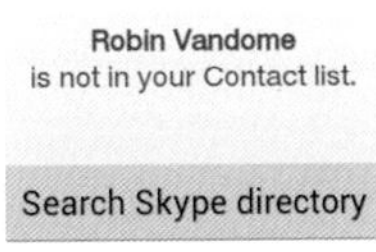

4. Matches for the requested person are shown. Tap on the **Add contacts** button to add them

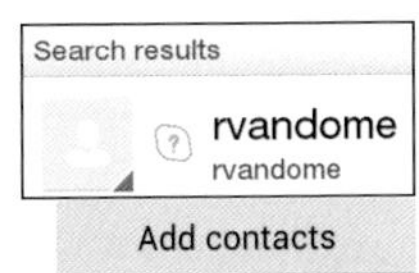

5. Tap on the **Add** button. The selected person will then be sent a Skype request and they have to accept it before they become a full contact

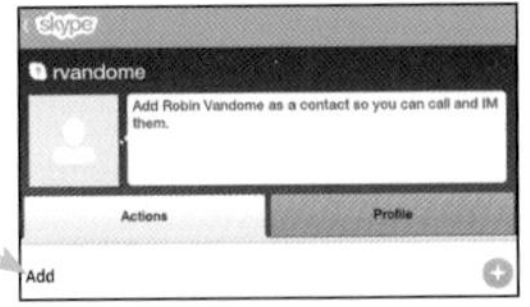

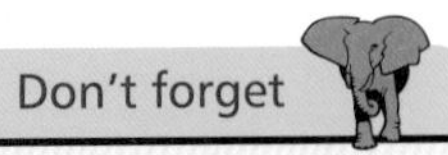

Once you add the Skype app to your Kindle Fire, your Skype contacts will also be available in your **Contacts** app.

Linking to social networks

Social networking sites are now an essential part in the way that people communicate and they can be linked directly to your Kindle Fire.

1. Swipe down from the top of the screen and tap on the **More** button and tap on the **My Account** button

2. Tap on the **Manage Social Network Accounts** button

3. Tap on one of the social networking options, e.g. Facebook or Twitter

4. Enter your sign in details for the selected social networking site and tap on the **Connect** button. This will give you direct access to your account

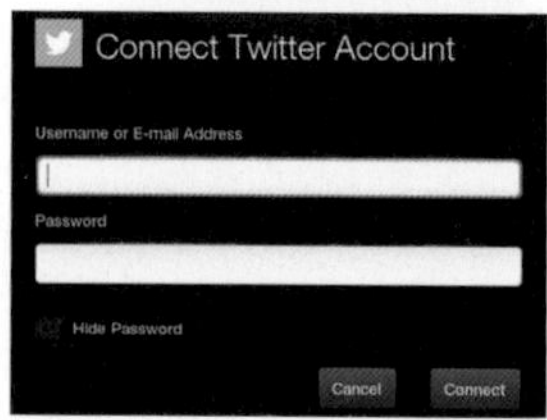

Beware

When you link to one of your social networking accounts you will be asked to give permission for Amazon to access the information in these accounts such as names, birthdays, email addresses and photos.

9 Don't get burnt

Security is a big issue for all forms of computing and this is no different for Kindle Fire users. This chapter looks at the issues of restricting access to inappropriate content, locking your Kindle Fire, restricting access to location-based services and privacy issues relating to your Kindle Fire and Amazon.

Parental Controls

With the massive amount of content available on the Web, and through items such as games, music, videos and books, it is always a concern that children, or grandchildren, may gain access to inappropriate material. With tablet computers it is even more of an issue, given the portable nature of these devices. But with your Kindle Fire it is possible to set Parental Controls so that certain types of content can be restricted.

1. Swipe down from the top of the screen, tap on the **More** button and tap on the **Parental Controls** button

2. Tap on the **On** button for **Parental Controls**

3. When you first set up Parental Controls you have to create a password. Tap on the **OK** button each time it is accessed

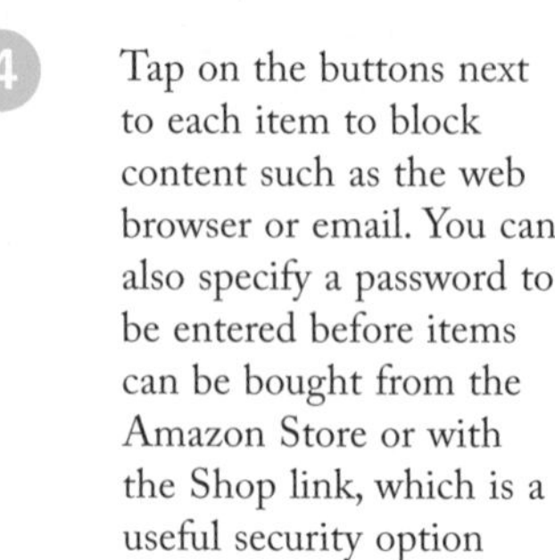

4. Tap on the buttons next to each item to block content such as the web browser or email. You can also specify a password to be entered before items can be bought from the Amazon Store or with the Shop link, which is a useful security option

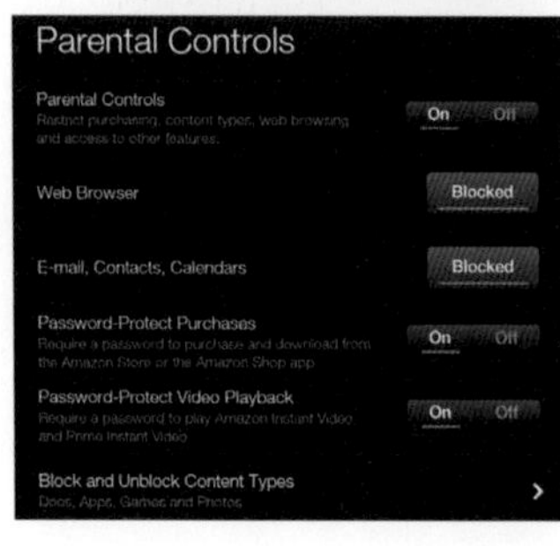

5. Tap on the **Block and Unblock Content Types** button to select content to block

Block and Unblock Content Types
Docs, Apps, Games and Photos

6. Tap on the buttons next to each item to block content for specific types, including Newsstand (newspapers and magazines), Books, Music, Video, Apps & Games and Photos

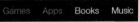

7. For each content type that has been blocked, the relevant button on the main Navigation Bar is grayed-out and cannot be accessed

8. The Parental Controls are also displayed in the Notifications area which is accessed by swiping down from the top of the screen

Don't forget

In the US there is also a free app called Kindle FreeTime that can be used by parents to customize the content that their children can view, such as specifying which books, apps, games and videos that they can access. Note, in the UK there is also a FreeTime app but this is for a different service.

Locking your Kindle Fire

If you are worried about anyone getting unauthorized access to your Kindle Fire, the best option can be to set a password for the Lock Screen so that it remains locked without the password. To do this:

1. Swipe down from the top of the screen, tap on the **More** button and tap on the **Security** button

2. Tap on the **On** button for **Lock-Screen Password**

3. Enter a password for the Lock Screen. Enter it again to confirm it and tap on the **Finish** button. This can be a four digit PIN or a longer, number-only, password

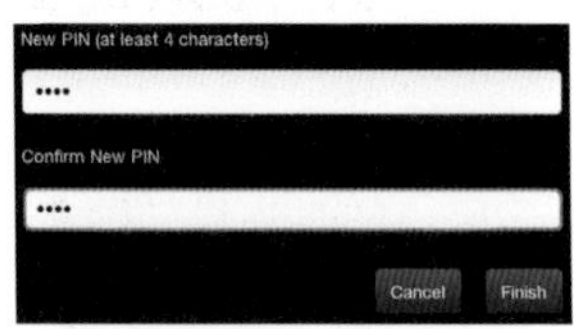

4. Swipe the padlock to the left to open the Lock Screen. Enter the password created in Step 3 and tap on the **OK** button to gain access to your Kindle Fire

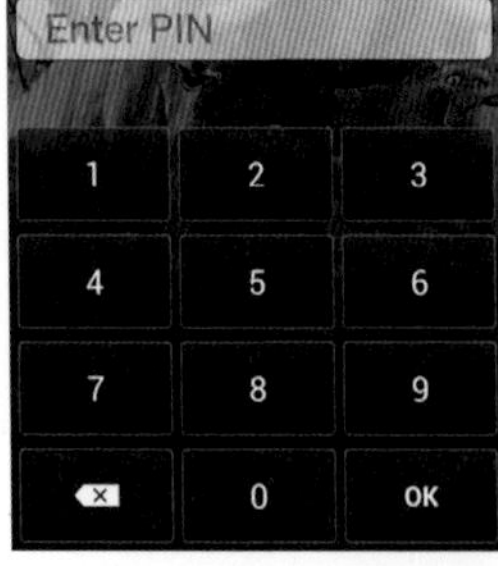

Location-Based Services

One concern with any online device is items getting unauthorised access to your files and folders. This is usually done by malicious software but people also have concerns about apps providing information from their Kindle Fire. This is done by Location-Based Services, whereby the apps provide location data to Amazon and third parties. At times this can be useful but you may also prefer to turn off this feature. To do this:

1. Swipe down from the top of the screen, tap on the **More** button and tap on the **Location-Based Services** button

Location-Based Services

2. Tap on the **Off** button for **Enable Location-Based Services**

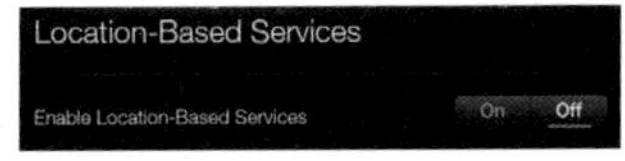

3. Tap on the **On** button to approve use of location information. Tap on the **OK** button if you want to provide this information to Amazon and third-parties via your apps

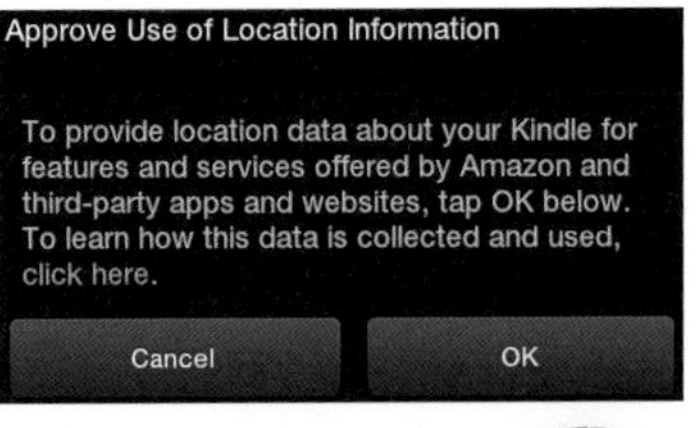

Beware

If you buy your Kindle Fire outside the US, or UK, you may not be able to use the full range of services, such as being able to download all music, apps and movies. Also, you should use your Amazon Account with a credit card registered in the country in which you are using it (US and UK).

Privacy issues

It is undeniable that the Kindle Fire is very tied-in to Amazon and its products and services. A lot of information that is used and entered into your Kindle Fire is made available to Amazon and it is only natural to want to know how this information is being used. Amazon provides details of this through pages on its website, which can be accessed directly from your Kindle Fire. To do this:

1. Swipe down from the top of the screen, tap on the **More** button and tap on the **Legal & Compliance** button

Legal & Compliance

2. Tap on the **Privacy** button. This takes you to the Amazon website

3. Tap on the **Amazon.com Privacy Notice** link

Amazon.com Privacy Notice

4. View the details of the Privacy Notice by clicking on the links in the bulleted list

Amazon.com Privacy Notice

Last updated: April 6, 2012. To see what has changed, click here.

Amazon.com knows that you care how information about you is used and shared, and we appreciate your trust that we will do so carefully and sensibly. This notice describes our privacy policy. **By visiting Amazon.com, you are accepting the practices described in this Privacy Notice.**

- What Personal Information About Customers Does Amazon.com Gather?
- What About Cookies?
- Does Amazon.com Share the Information It Receives?
- How Secure Is Information About Me?
- What About Third-Party Advertisers and Links to Other Websites?
- Which Information Can I Access?
- What Choices Do I Have?
- Are Children Allowed to Use Amazon.com?
- Does Amazon.com Participate in the Safe Harbor Program?

Beware

There have been some concerns expressed about the ease with which items can be ordered from Amazon with the Kindle Fire. An Amazon Account password is not required as you are already logged in via your Amazon Kindle *(correct at the time of printing)*.